Getting to Know You!

Social Skills Curriculum
for Grades 4 & 5

by
Dennis Hanken, Ed.S.
and
Judith Kennedy, Ed.S.

ISBN No. 0-932796-88-5

Library of Congress Catalog No. 98-72122

Publisher—

Educational Media Corporation®
Box 21311
Minneapolis, MN 55421
(612) 781-0088

Production Editor—

Don L. Sorenson

Graphic Designer—

Earl R. Sorenson

Dedication

This book is dedicated to the researchers and authors who preceded us in the study of social skills and in writing programs to assist with teaching social skills components. This book is also dedicated to the teachers and children who have shown us that our curriculum is effective, fun, and easy to use.

About the Authors

Dennis Hanken and his wife, Wendy, are the parents of three daughters. He has polished his own social skills and developed an awareness of the need for social skills training in his 28 years working with youth in an educational setting. His fellow workers and students enjoy his keen sense of humor, empathy, and enjoyment of life. He is currently a school psychologist in the Rapid City School System in South Dakota.

Judith Kennedy is married and the parent of two children, two stepchildren, a daughter-in-law, and a grandson. A focus of her life has always been to assist children to interact respectfully, live their lives fully, and achieve their potential. She has thirty years experience working with youth and is currently a school psychologist and Licensed Professional Counselor.

Acknowledgments

We thank Marcene Rand, Beth Steen, Wendy Hanken, and LuAnn Mattern for their assistance and creativity.

Thanks also to the "Dear Wally" publishers, Guideposts Book Division, 16 East 34th Street, New York, NY 10016, for the use of "Dear Wally" letters to support our curriculum.

Table of Contents

Dennis Hanken, Ed.S. and Judith Kennedy, Ed.S.

Foreword

This is the second volume of *Getting To Know You: Social Skills Curriculum*. The first volume presents the curriculum for first through grade three. That volume was so positively received that we researched and developed this curriculum for grades four and five.

Like the first volume, this one is based on the best practices of establishing the need, modeling the skill, role playing with feedback using "Think Aloud" strategies, and assigning activities to generalize the skill into other environments. Each lesson plan states the objective of that lesson and gives an activity to help your students see why it is an important skill to learn.

First, you model the skill using "Think Aloud" strategies, which are also reinforced on the posters for each lesson. Your students role play the skill using different scenarios and incorporating the "Think Aloud" strategies. Activities are included to be done in other settings in the school, at home or in the community, and with peers in order to generalize this skill to other areas of your students' lives.

We also include a "Materials Needed" section to alert you to what materials you may need that are not included in the textbook. We have included a pre/post test for you to use if you want to measure the skill acquisition for an individual student or the class. A letter to the parents is included so you may inform parents of the curriculum and what your students will learn.

Our curriculum is based on a prosocial model, which supports the belief that inappropriate behavior may be the result of inadequate social skills, and that social skills can be taught just like any academic subject. Our curriculum teaches new skills rather than correcting or punishing maladaptive behavior. *Getting to Know You!* is designed for use in the classroom by teachers or counselors.

The curriculum may be taught daily until the skill is learned, and then the skill may be reinforced on an as-needed basis. This curriculum is well researched and designed to be user friendly. All students can benefit from learning these skill components, and the skills are particularly useful for those students who are isolated or who are newly included in the regular classroom.

We intend our curriculum to be easy and fun to use. Our hope is that you will have fun with it.

Dennis Hanken

Judith Kennedy

Instructions

1. This curriculum is based on well-researched practices. One of the reasons for its documented success is the "Think Aloud" strategies. These strategies are actually the internal dialogue we recommend be taught to students. The consistent use of the "Think Aloud" strategies by all school staff provides the basis for the success of this curriculum in decreasing undesirable behavior, while increasing the desired social skills. You will have better success changing the behavior of your students if all personnel are trained to use the common language in the "Think Aloud" strategies. This includes principals, secretarial staff, lunchroom and playground personnel, and auxiliary staff.

2. The posters reinforce the "Think Aloud" strategies. They follow each lesson and should be enlarged and displayed in the classrooms, hallways, and other areas of your school. Copy the student awards at the end of each section and present them to your students to reinforce the skills learned.

3. Each lesson has a story, activity, or discussion to "Establish the Need." Additional stories or activities under "Extended Activities" also will reinforce the skill in the lesson.

4. There is a sample letter to the parents should you choose to elicit parental support prior to beginning this curriculum.

5. This curriculum is based on the teaching methods of modeling the skill, providing opportunity for the students to role play, and reinforcing their skills with feedback. It is important that you actually model the desired skill using the "Think Aloud" strategies so your students can see the desired behavior.

6. The role play section of each lesson is meant to provide an opportunity for your students to practice the desired skill. This is the time to give feedback and correct any behavior. Research results are inconclusive as to whether role playing an incorrect example of each behavior is helpful for the students in learning the desired behavior. Some of the leaders in the field of social skill development believe that students learn the desired skill better if they are able to practice the contrast behavior; other feel this is unnecessary and a distraction. We have sometimes included a contrast role play under "Helpful Hints." You may use it at your discretion, knowing the needs of your students.

7. The most common reason for the failure of a social skills curriculum is in the lack of those skills generalizing to other environments. We correct this by providing "Transfer Training" activities to be done in other environments.

8. We hope you enjoy this curriculum, have fun with it, and use your own creativity to expand the lessons. We believe that for it to be the most effective, the skills should be taught in the order presented.

Screening Checklist
Teacher's Checklist

_____   _____   _____
Student's Name   Rated By   Date

Directions:

Circle the appropriate letter for each question. Rate this child in comparison with other children in the class.

Key:

5—**Very often**—means daily occurrence

3—**Sometimes**—means 2 to 3 times a week

1—**Seldom**—means 0 occurrence

I. Classroom Skills

1. Does the student listen to instructions or directions?	5	4	3	2	1
2. Does the student complete assignments on time?	5	4	3	2	1
3. Does the student follow classroom rules?	5	4	3	2	1
4. Does the student cooperate with a work partner?	5	4	3	2	1
5. Is the student prepared for class?	5	4	3	2	1

II. Interpersonal Relationships

1. Is the student accepted by most of his or her classmates?	5	4	3	2	1
2. Does the student have one or more friends?	5	4	3	2	1
3. Is the student often a victim of teasing?	5	4	3	2	1
4. Is the student respectful of other's property?	5	4	3	2	1
5. Is the student excluded by his or her peers?	5	4	3	2	1

III. Identifying and Expressing Feelings

1. Can the student express feelings in an appropriate way?	5	4	3	2	1
2. Does the student show understanding of other's feelings?	5	4	3	2	1
3. Does the student express unusual or extreme feelings?	5	4	3	2	1

IV. Relieving Stress

1. Can the student accept losing or failing?	5	4	3	2	1
2. Does the student handle changes in the daily routine?	5	4	3	2	1
3. Does the student over or under react to conflict?	5	4	3	2	1
4. Does the student show signs of anxiety, nervousness, or stress?	5	4	3	2	1
5. Does the student defend his or her rights?	5	4	3	2	1

V. Problem Solving/Decision Making

1. Does the student accept responsibility for his or her actions?	5	4	3	2	1
2. Is the student able to make a decision independently?	5	4	3	2	1
3. Does the student overreact to minor problems?	5	4	3	2	1

VI. Replacement Skills for Aggression

1. Does the student express anger appropriately?	5	4	3	2	1
2. Does the student avoid fights?	5	4	3	2	1
3. Does the student work out problems with friends by talking and compromising?	5	4	3	2	1
4. Does the student avoid situations which may cause problems?	5	4	3	2	1

VII. Self-Acceptance

1. Does the student like himself or herself?	5	4	3	2	1
2. Does the student avoid putting down self and others?	5	4	3	2	1
3. Does the student tolerate differences in others?	5	4	3	2	1

Dennis Hanken, Ed.S. and Judith Kennedy, Ed.S.

Our Class is Studying Social Skills!

Dear Parents:

Our class is beginning a social skills curriculum. Your child will be learning better ways to resolve conflict, make friends, and follow rules. These skills will help your child feel better about himself or herself, make decisions, handle stress and choose the best action in a given situation. Our belief is that in teaching children appropriate social skills, there is less need for correction of behavior.

We ask that you help reinforce these social skills at home. For each lesson there will be an activity to do at home. The purpose of these activities is to help your child do these skills in any environment.

There are seven areas of skills your child will learn with specific lessons under each area. The seven areas are:

1. Innovative Classroom Skills
2. Interpersonal Relationships/Friendship—Making Skills
3. Identifying and Expressing Feelings
4. Relieving Stress
5. Problem Solving/Decision Making
6. Replacement Skills to Aggression
7. Self-Esteem/Self-Acceptance

Thank you for your support. Please call me if you have any concerns or questions.

Classroom Teacher

Lesson 1:   Being Prepared for Class

Objective: Students will have appropriate materials and be ready to participate in class.

Materials Needed: Student materials for the chosen class, copies of the "Homework Form," page 15.

Establish the Need: Dialogue about students preparing for school and class. Read the following story: *"Matt always got to school just as the bell rang. He didn't get up in time for breakfast and often forgot his book bag at home. Today was the class field trip to the geological museum. Matt did not remember his lunch, his permission slip, nor his homework to be turned in before going."* Discuss: What might be the consequences for Matt?

Procedures:

Step 1: Model the skill:

Model using "Think Aloud" strategies—getting ready for social studies.

1. What materials do I need?
2. Do I need paper, pencil, book?
3. Do I have homework?
4. Gather the necessary items.
5. Be ready to start.

Helpful Hints: Dialogue: What you need to do to be prepared to teach each day.

Step 2: Role play with feedback:

A. Students demonstrate how each one prepares for a certain class.

B. In pairs, have them role play being prepared for class.

Helpful Hints: Your students learn organizational tips from each other by seeing how each person gets prepared. Role play what happens to students who are not prepared for class.

Step 3: Transfer training:

A. **School:** Have the music or art teacher reinforce being prepared for class.

B. **Home/Community:** The students, with their parents, list the things they need as they prepare to leave home for school.

C. **Peers:** Students itemize the things they need for an overnight stay with a friend.

Comments: Some students may need one-on-one assistance to approach organizing their materials. Contracts, specified times each day for organizing materials, containers for a specified item, and organizational checklists would all be helpful.

Extended Activities: (1) Students relate how their parents prepare for their jobs. (2) Draw a picture showing the items you need to be prepared to go on a weekend trip with your family. (3) Have your students prepare organizational systems for their desks. "Homework Form," page 14 and "Classroom Skills Award," page 15.

Lesson 1:   Being Prepared for Class

1. What materials do I need?

2. Do I need paper, pencil, book?

3. Do I have homework?

4. Gather the necessary items.

5. Be ready to start.

CLASSROOM SKILLS

Homework Form

Student _____

Date _____

Skill: _____

"Think Aloud" strategies used: _____

_____

_____

With whom will I do this skill? _____

_____

When? _____

What was the result? _____

_____

How did I do?_____

_____

Classroom
Skills Award
to

_____

for mastering the skill of

_____

Date _____

Teacher signature _____

Lesson 2: Listening

Objective: Students will listen to the teacher or peers when giving information to the class.

Materials Needed: None.

Establish the Need: Discuss and elicit responses about what would happen if students didn't listen to the rules of a new game, the instructions to follow for a fire drill, or the instructions parents leave for you as a baby-sitter.

Procedures:

Step 1: Model the skill:

A. With an adult or student, model using "Think Aloud" strategies—how to listen to another person.

    1. *Look* at the person.

    2. *Sit quietly*.

    3. *Think* about what the person is saying.

Step 2: Role play with feedback:

A. Have student volunteers teach other students a new game or magic trick. Give feedback on how the class members listened.

B. In groups of 4 or 5, one person whispers a short story to another person and that person passes it on. What happened to the story by the time it reached the last person?

Helpful Hints: Listening is a crucial skill which causes even adults difficulty. Students are more likely to listen to others if they are listened to. Keep this in mind when your students talk to you. Pretend you don't listen when children talk or vice versa. Discuss frustrations.

Step 3: Transfer training:

A. **School:** Ask another teacher to model and reinforce the "Listening" lesson.

B. **Home/Community:** Assign the homework of listening to a family member. Report back.

C. **Peers:** In pairs for one recess, your students should take turns talking and then listening. Class discussion after recess.

Helpful Hints: Your students need to remember that communicating requires a person to alternate talking and listening.

Comments: Your students will be better able to listen if listening periods are broken up by other activities. In spite of seeming passive, listening takes a lot of energy.

Extended Activities: (1) Students prepare skits showing good listening skills. (2) These skits could be put on for lower grade classrooms working on listening. (3) Your students could list all the good/poor listening examples they see in one week. "Homework Form," page 14 and "Classroom Skills Award," page 16.

Lesson 2: Listening

1. *Look* at the person.

2. *Sit* quietly.

3. *Think* about what the person is saying.

CLASSROOM SKILLS

Lesson 3: Following Oral Directions

Objective: Students will correctly follow multistep oral directions.

Materials Needed: None.

Establish the Need: Give the example of being lost in an unfamiliar neighborhood and asking for directions. Discuss what techniques you use for remembering multistep directions.

Procedures:

Step 1: Model the skill:

Model using "Think Aloud" strategies—listening to a 5-step direction.

1. Listen.
2. What do I do first, second, third?
3. Do I understand?
4. Do it.

Helpful Hints: You might share techniques you use for remembering multistep directions.

Step 2: Role play with feedback:

A. Give 5-step directions by row or group. Give feedback.

B. Give directions to your house from your school. Discuss.

Helpful Hints: Students could share techniques they use to remember oral directions. What would happen if you forget CPR techniques and someone has a heart attack? Discuss.

Step 3: Transfer training:

A. **School:** Ask the P.E. teacher to give 5-step directions and feedback to students on how they did.

B. **Home/Community:** Have each student orally give directions to his or her home from the school.

C. **Peers:** Pair or group students for board games. Have one student give directions and others listen.

Comments: It is helpful to use a multi-modal approach for directions, i.e., write on the board as well as give oral directions.

Extended Activities: Have your students in groups design a new game for the class to play. They will give directions orally. Discuss the success of the class in listening to directions. "Homework Form," page 14 and "Classroom Skills Award," page 15.

Lesson 3: Following Oral Directions

1. *Listen*.
2. What do I do first, second, third?

1. _____
2. _____
3. _____

3. Do I understand?
4. *Do it*.

CLASSROOM SKILLS

Classroom Skills *(sidebar)*

Lesson 4: Following Written Directions

Objective: Students will read directions and follow them accurately.

Materials Needed: Worksheets with unusual directions; chalkboard.

Establish the Need: Show some anonymous papers which are incorrect because of a failure to follow directions. Ask your students to share experiences where they were penalized for not following directions.

Procedures:

Step 1: Model the skill:

Model using "Think Aloud" strategies—following written directions.

1. Read the directions.
2. Do I understand them?
3. Clarify with your teacher if needed.
4. Do what the directions say.

Helpful Hints: It will help to be consistent in requiring your students to read directions before starting work and reinforcing those students who do so.

Step 2: Role play with feedback:

A. Write directions for an art project on the board. Use one that requires 5 to 6 steps that must be done in order. It could be paper folding, papier-mache, collage, and so forth.

B. Role play following classroom rules that are on a poster in the classroom.

Helpful Hints: Students who are impulsive will tend to jump in and begin work before reading the instructions. They need guidance to see why they must consistently read the directions. Give your students wrong directions on a worksheet. Did they recognize this? Discuss.

Step 3: Transfer training:

A. **School:** Ask the computer teacher to use a program that requires students to read and follow directions before they can work it.

B. **Home/Community:** Ask the parents to have the students cook a simple dish, i.e., macaroni and cheese, which requires them to read directions.

C. **Peers:** Divide in groups, have your students write directions for each other to follow.

Comments: Students who have reading difficulties may feel penalized because even though they read the directions, they are unable to follow them accurately. It would be good to team them with others to enable them to get the support they need.

Extended Activities: (1) In groups, students write the directions for an activity. Trade these activities with other groups. (2) In groups, students follow written directions to do an activity such as no-bake cookies or making play dough. (3) With map handouts, have the students trail the path of a traveler following the written directions. "Homework Form," page 14 and "Classroom Skills Award," page 15.

Lesson 4:   Following Written Directions

1. Read the directions.

2. Do I understand them?

3. Clarify with your teacher if needed.

4. Do what the directions say.

CLASSROOM SKILLS

Lesson 5: Ignoring Distractions

Objective: Students will continue working despite visual, auditory, or other distractions.

Materials Needed: Radio or tape.

Establish the Need: Discuss what distractions are: visual, auditory, tactile, or olfactory. Discuss and have your students submit suggestions for ignoring distractions. Define *distractions* and *ignore*. Discuss what conditions you need to work comfortably.

Procedures:

Step 1: Model the skill:

Model using "Think Aloud" strategies—ignoring.

1. What is distracting me?
2. How can I work despite the distractions?
   a. Ignore.
   b. Move to a quiet area.
   c. Put up a carrel.
3. Keep working.

Helpful Hints: Some ways to avoid distractions: Provide a quiet area in your room for working. Earphones, timers, and a predetermined teacher signal can all help students stay on task.

Step 2: Role play with feedback:

A. Students work on worksheets with loud radio on for two minutes. Discuss.

B. Have them work on a worksheet in a quiet classroom for two minutes. Reward your students for on-task behavior.

Helpful Hints: Students are off-task sometimes because the work level or amount is overwhelming. Curriculum-based assessment can help determine their skill level. Assignments may need to be shortened. When everyone is talking, is it hard to concentrate?

Step 3: Transfer training:

A. **School:** Ask the music teacher to assist in reinforcing students who stay on task and ignore distractions.

B. **Home/Community:** Assign a worksheet to be done at home. Do part of the worksheet in a quiet area and part in a noisy area. Discuss the results.

C. **Peers:** In cooperative learning groups, have your students work on a relevant academic area. Rotate and reward the students who are ignoring distractions.

Comments: For a child who is extremely distractible, you may want to involve the school psychologist to see if ADHD is the concern.

Extended Activities: (1) Students create a skit showing various ways to ignore distractions. (2) Have them create drawings showing various distractions and ways to ignore them. "Homework Form," page 14 and "Classroom Skills Award," page 15.

Lesson 5: Ignoring Distractions

1. What is distracting me?

2. How can I work despite the distractions?

a. Ignore.

b. Move to a quiet area.

c. Put up a carrel.

3. Keep working.

CLASSROOM SKILLS

Lesson 6: Completing Your Assignments

Objective: Students will complete assignments.

Materials Needed: Worksheets, Learning Centers.

Establish the Need: Discuss with your students what would happen if you, as the teacher, did not complete your class schedule in time to get them to lunch. Lead a discussion in what happens if they haven't completed getting ready when it is time for their family to leave.

Procedures:

Step 1: Model the skill:

Model using "Think Aloud" strategies—completing an assignment.

1. What do I need to do?
2. Do I have everything I need to start?
3. Start working.
4. Keep working until the assignment is done.

Helpful Hints: It is important to have the work amount realistic to the student's ability.

Step 2: Role play with feedback:

A. Give out realistic worksheets. Obtain student feedback in the amount of time needed to complete the worksheet. Set a timer. The students finishing early may go to a Learning Center or read.

Helpful Hints: Finishing work is a huge task for some students. Individual contracts may help in cases where motivation is the problem. Modified work can help if the skill level is the problem.

Step 3: Transfer training:

A. **School:** Request teachers of other subjects to reinforce completing assignments.

B. **Home/Community:** Ask parents to reinforce completing work by praising the child for one chore completed.

C. **Peers:** Students who finish work early may help those who have difficulty with completing work.

Helpful Hints: Parents often have as much trouble at home with work completion. You may want to conference with them for ideas and consistency.

Comments: It is important to be sensitive to each student in assigning work amounts. Some students will be overwhelmed by the level or amount of work to be done. Students with ADD characteristics may have a difficult time getting started. Reinforce those students for getting started.

Extended Activities: (1) Assign a project to be done in groups in a certain amount of time. This could be a poster, a skit, or a poem—whatever supports your current curriculum. Each member needs to be responsible for some part. (2) Assign each student a different part of a chapter in a book to read. Then each student will report on the portion read rather than read entire chapter. Set time limits. "Homework Form," page 14 and "Classroom Skills Award," page 15.

Lesson 6:   Completing Your Assignments

1. What do I need to do?

2. Do I have everything I need to start?

3. Start working.

4. Keep working until the assignment is done.

CLASSROOM SKILLS

Classroom Skills

Lesson 7: Making Relevant Remarks During Class Discussions

Objective: Students will participate with relevant remarks during class discussion.

Materials Needed: None.

Establish the Need: Discuss with your students what would happen if everyone talked at once, if only 4 or 5 people in class ever added to the discussion, and if some students never participated.

Procedures:

Step 1: Model the skill:

With another adult or a student, model using "Think Aloud" strategies—how to contribute relevant remarks to a discussion.

1. Listen to the discussion.
2. What can I add?
3. Take turns talking.
4. Stay on the subject.

Helpful Hints: For some children it is more of a problem to get them to contribute. Draw them out by showing you accept what they have to say and redirect rather than criticize a mistake.

Step 2: Role play with feedback:

A. Put your students in groups and have them discuss an upcoming or recent event, holiday, sport activity, movie, and so forth. Ensure that all students are participating.

B. Role play appropriate comments during a math class. Discuss.

Helpful Hints: Solicit children who dominate discussions to help draw out those students who rarely contribute. Discuss what happens when remarks are irrelevant.

Step 3: Transfer training:

A. **School:** Ask teachers to reinforce participating in discussions with relevant remarks.

B. **Home/Community:** Ask parents to discuss a topic one time a week at the dinner table or family meeting and to seek everyone's participation.

C. **Peers:** Assign students to spend one recess with a peer from the class and have a discussion. Discuss the results after recess.

Comments: Some students will be afraid to contribute to discussions because of past embarrassment. Help them overcome this by encouraging responses and supporting their attempts.

Extended Activities: (1) Using volunteers, students lead the class in a discussion of a relevant topic of interest. (2) Have them submit ideas to help everyone participate in class discussions. "Homework Form," page 14 and "Classroom Skills Award," page 15.

Lesson 7:   Making Relevant Remarks During Class Discussion

1. Listen to the discussion.

2. What can I add?

3. Take turns talking.

4. Stay on the subject.

CLASSROOM SKILLS

Classroom Skills

Lesson 8: Interrupting

Objective: Students will participate in discussions without interrupting.

Materials Needed: Puppets.

Establish the Need: With puppets (you can use student volunteers), show what happens when people interrupt and do not listen to each other.

Procedures:

Step 1: Model the skill:

A. Model using "Think Aloud" strategies—taking turns talking.

    1. Listen to the other person.

    2. Wait until the person is done talking.

    3. Raise my hand, if necessary, or say, "Excuse me."

    4. Talk.

Helpful Hints: There is interrupting in class discussions and in small groups or pairs. Handle both types of situations by helping students to take their turn.

Step 2: Role play with feedback:

A. Using puppets, have your students discuss a topic of common interest by taking turns and not interrupting.

B. Role play interrupting in a group of adults. Role play in groups. Discuss how it feels to be interrupted.

Helpful Hints: You can show a good example of the correct way to interrupt in the class. Practice interrupting in a sarcastic way and discuss the results.

Step 3: Transfer training:

A. **School:** Ask the P.E. teacher to reinforce this lesson by giving feedback to students on correct ways to interrupt.

B. **Home/Community:** A brother or sister is on the phone and you need to call. How do you interrupt?

C. **Peers:** Arrange your students in groups to plan a fictitious event, i.e., party, with specific instructions on practicing interrupting correctly.

Comments: You may also want to include teaching students to not interrupt in a casual conversation, but to wait their turn and take turns talking.

Extended Activities: (1) Students create a skit using puppets to present the correct way of interrupting to lower grade classrooms. (2) Students design games which focus on correct interrupting, i.e., you cannot talk unless you are holding the baton or ball of yarn. "Homework Form," page 14 and "Classroom Skills Award," page 15.

Lesson 8:   Interrupting

1. Listen to the other person.

2. Wait until the person is done talking.

3. Raise my hand, if necessary, or say, "Excuse me."

4. Talk.

CLASSROOM SKILLS

Lesson 9: Following Classroom Rules

Objective: Students will adhere to rules in various classroom settings.

Materials Needed: Poster of rules in your class.

Establish the Need: Talk about traffic lights and what would happen if we didn't have them. Solicit other examples from your students.

Procedures:

Step 1: Model the skill:

Model using "Think Aloud" strategies—following rules of the class.

1. Read the rules.
2. Do I understand what they mean?
3. Will I have problems following the rules—realizing consequences?
4. Try to follow the rules the best I can.

Helpful Hints: It is best to keep your rules brief, few in number and written in a positive format.

Step 2: Role play with feedback:

A. Go over each rule of the class and have your students demonstrate their understanding by performing each.

B. Role play following class rules.

Helpful Hints: It would be beneficial to role play the rules of other classes and discuss the variations, if any. What happens when you don't follow classroom rules? Discuss.

Step 3: Transfer training:

A. **School:** Ask the lunchroom and playground personnel to give your students feedback on following the rules in those settings.

B. **Home/Community:** A homework assignment of every student is to check with their parents and report back what the home rules are.

C. **Peers:** In groups of 4, students discuss rules in their homes.

Comments: For some students it is a thrill to "get away" with not following the rules. These students need assistance in developing an internal focus of control so they are not resisting what they perceive as external control.

Extended Activities: (1) In groups, students make up poster lists of rules they think should be classroom rules. Discuss. (2) Students will make a rap song using classroom rules. "Homework Form," page 14 and "Classroom Skills Award," page 15.

Lesson 9:   Following Classroom Rules

1. Read the rules.

2. Do I understand what they mean?

3. Will I have problems following the rules— realizing consequences?

4. Try to follow the rules the best I can.

CLASSROOM SKILLS

Classroom Skills *(vertical side tab)*

Lesson 10: Cooperating with a Work Partner

Objective: Students will share materials and work cooperatively with a partner or partners during a class activity.

Materials Needed: Supplies for an art project (poster board, magic markers, magazines, glue).

Establish the Need: Read the stories, "No Cooperation—No Gain!" and "Negative Partners," on the following page.

Procedures:

Step 1: Model the skill:

Model using "Think Aloud" strategies—how to cooperate.

1. Share materials.
2. Decide who does what.
3. Listen to their ideas and voice mine.
4. Work until done.

Helpful Hints: Your students may need some assistance in organizing themselves.

Step 2: Role play with feedback:

A. Assign your students in pairs or groups to complete a picture of a relevant scene: upcoming holiday, drawing of buildings they both know, drawing of a beaver dam, and so forth.

B. Assign partners to a long-term project (9 weeks).

Helpful Hints: Rotate to ensure the job responsibilities are shared. Give feedback on the amount of time left for the project. What happens when you don't cooperate with your work partner?

Step 3: Transfer training:

A. **School:** Ask the P.E. teacher to have your students assigned to teams to share equipment to play a sport. (Softball, basketball, etc.)

B. **Home/Community:** Ask parents to arrange a chore that needs to be done with someone else.

C. **Peers:** Assign your students in groups for recess where they need to share equipment like balls, bars, and so forth. Discuss.

Comments: This is a skill needed for life success and should be reinforced daily. More people lose their jobs because of work habits than skill level.

Extended Activities: (1) Assign your students in groups to make a papier-mache item or a mobile. Reinforce cooperative working. (2) Give groups of students a large piece of paper. Then give directions for drawing a person. Each person draws a part and hands paper to next person. Hang it up when it is done and compare the results. *Directions*: Draw a head big as a pumpkin, make a neck long and thin, make a belly round and fat, make 2 arms long and burly, make 2 legs thick and stout, add 2 feet sticking out to the sides, put 2 eyes looking to the left, add a long nose with a ball on the end, put on 2 ears shaped like butterfly wings, add a mouth with a toothless grin. To finish, add 3 hairs spiraling up from the head. "Homework Form," page 14 and "Classroom Skills Award," page 15.

No Cooperation—No Gain!

"Marty and Jim needed to make a castle for their social studies class. Marty wanted to design the castle after one he had seen in Germany. Jim had other ideas. Marty would not listen to Jim. They argued and argued. When it came time to hand in their project, they hadn't started."

1. What happens when you don't cooperate?
2. What does "cooperate" mean?

Negative Partners

"Danny and Debbie were science partners. They were not good friends. Danny wanted to be the boss and tell Debbie what to do. Debbie decided to tell the teacher about Danny's bossiness and lack of cooperation."

1. How do you feel when one person is the boss all the time?
2. Should Debbie tell the teacher or ask Danny not to be bossy first?

Lesson 10: Cooperating with a Work Partner

1. Share materials.

2. Decide who does what.

3. Listen to their ideas and voice mine.

4. Work until done.

CLASSROOM SKILLS

Lesson 11: Initiating a Conversation

Objective: Students will be able to start a conversation with peers and adults.

Materials Needed: Blackboard.

Establish the Need: Knowing what to say to others is often difficult to do. It is sometimes more difficult with the opposite sex. If you are nice to someone and start with short conversations, this will have positive results. Read the stories, "Taking a Risk" and "A Happy Ending," on the next page. One student could read Lisa's part and another Bob's.

Procedures:

Step 1: Model the skill:

Select a person with whom to talk. Model the "Think Aloud" strategies—

1. Is this a good time?
2. What should I say first?
3. Look at the person and say "Hi" or "Good morning."
4. Is the other person listening?
5. Should I continue to talk?

Helpful Hints: If your first time "flops," try again. It gets easier each time. Or, try a new approach.

Step 2: Role play with feedback:

A. Have your students brainstorm different ways to start a conversation.

1. Boy to boy.
2. Girl to girl.
3. Boy to girl.
4. Girl to boy.

B. Take turns role playing the four types of pairs. Rotate and give feedback.

Helpful Hints: What happens when you say something to people and they don't respond or walk away? Discuss.

Step 3: Transfer training:

A. **School:** Practice starting conversations with staff and the principal.

B. **Home/Community:** Students start conversations as a homework assignment with people they don't know, but would like to, in their neighborhoods.

C. **Peers:** Start a conversation with a boy or girl you would like to get to know better.

Comments: Starting a conversation with people is a skill that requires practice and refinement.

Extended Activities: Using compliments is a good way to start a conversation. Students tell the story about "How you met your best friend." Emphasize the first conversation you had with that person. Do a sociogram. "Friendship Award," page 37 and "Homework Form," page 14.

Taking a Risk

Bob, one of the students in fifth grade, wants to talk to a nice girl, Lisa. Bob is somewhat shy, but he decides to take a chance. Monday morning is rather dull just before school starts. All the girls are chatting about the weekend and the boys are talking about the big basketball game next Wednesday. Lisa drifts over by the boys with her girlfriend, Kate. Bob sees Lisa coming and says to himself, "Is this the right time? What should I say? I'll just say 'hi' and see what happens."

"Hi Lisa," says Bob. Lisa hesitates and says, "Hi" and waits for Bob to say more. Bob knows Lisa is listening and waiting, Bob says, "Did you have a good weekend?" Lisa says, "It was okay, nothing special." Bob continues to talk and listen to Lisa. The bell rings and Bob and Lisa line up. Bob thinks to himself, "I am glad I took a risk and said hello. It was really easy after that."

A Happy Ending

Jill is a new girl in fifth grade. She decides to go to a baseball game, even though she doesn't know any boy on the team. She thinks she recognizes one of the boys, Roger, a boy in her class.

After the game Jill decides to take a risk and she says to Roger, "Nice Game." He replies, "Thanks. Who are you?" She replies, "I just moved here from another state." "Well, that's great. Would you like to split a candy bar at the convenience store?" "Sure. Let's go."

1. Starting a conversation is a risk.
2. These two stories have good endings. When two strangers meet each other, is the end result always like this story?

Friendship Award

to

_____

for using the skill of

_____

Date _____

_____

Lesson 11: Initiating a Conversation

1. Is this is a good time?

2. What should I say first?

3. Look at the person and say "Hi" or "Good Morning."

4. Is the other person listening?

5. Should I continue to talk?

FRIENDSHIP SKILLS

Lesson 12: Putting Closure to a Conversation

Objective: Students will learn to put closure on a conversation in a socially acceptable way.

Materials Needed: None.

Establish the Need: It is important to listen to people and complete a conversation because people feel important when you listen. Brainstorm a list on how to conclude a conversation. Set up a demonstration with students using the brainstorm list. Demonstrate how to end a conversation on the phone. Read the stories, "A Helping Conversation" and "Poor Listener," on the following page.

Procedures:

Step 1: Model the skill:

A. Using "Think Aloud" strategies, have your students model starting a conversation, staying with the conversation, and putting closure to the conversation.

1. Say what I need to say.
2. Give the other person a chance to respond.
3. Listen and respond to what other the person said.
4. Make a closing remark such as, "I need to go" or "I'm late, excuse me."

Helpful Hints: Teaching children how to be brief about things that happen in life helps. Your students need to know when to talk in detail.

Step 2: Role play with feedback:

A. Pair your students for practice starting and ending conversations.

B. Provide feedback and suggestions.

C. Assign your students to small groups (3 to 4) and have them practice leaving the group and excusing themselves.

Helpful Hints: Talk about how difficult it is leaving a game or a group early. What about: peer pressure, responsibilities, and leaving when you are having fun. Discuss ending a conversation inappropriately. People might think you are rude and a snob.

Step 3: Transfer training:

A. **School:** Practice ending conversations before school starts, at lunch, or before class starts.

B. **Home/Community:** Practice ending conversations at home with your parents or siblings.

C. **Peers:** Practice ending a conversation at the mall, a friend's house, or on the phone.

Comments: Your students need to know how to talk on the phone and end those conversations appropriately.

Extended Activities: Students at this age are invited for sleepovers, birthday parties, and other social gatherings. It is important for them to feel confident in order to be appropriate. Practice using different settings, beginning and ending a conversation.

Educational Media Corporation®, Box 21311, Minneapolis, MN 55421-0311

Friendship Skills

A Helping Conversation

Tony called his best friend, Pete, on the phone. "Hi Pete, how are you doing?" "Fine," says Pete, "What are you doing?" Tony responds, "Doing my homework. What about you?" "The same." "I am stuck," says Pete. "Can you help me with 12 on page 47 in math?" "Sure, try it this way." "Thanks a lot," says Pete. "Oh, I have to get off the phone and do the dishes. Thanks for calling and helping me out." "No problem," say Tony, "What are friends for? See you tomorrow." (Click)

1. Did they end the conversation appropriately?
2. What are some other ways to end a conversation?

Poor Listener

Kathy, the chatter queen of fourth grade, talked about everyone in class. She was also loud and she never listened to her classmates.

1. Do you think Kathy had any friends?
2. What suggestions could Kathy use about rumors, listening, conversations, or being polite?

Lesson 12: Putting Closure to a Conversation

1. Say what I need to say.

2. Give the other person a chance to respond.

3. Listen and respond to what the other person said.

4. Make a closing remark such as, "I need to go" or "I'm late, excuse me."

FRIENDSHIP SKILLS

Lesson 13: Asking a Question

Objective: Students will be able to ask a question confidently, knowing that is the right time and the right place.

Materials Needed: Blackboard.

Establish the Need: Asking appropriate questions requires good timing and good listening skills. Set up a scenario for asking questions in a group or one-on-one. Discuss different ways to ask a question. List these, i.e., "I don't understand this part?" "Could you repeat the directions?" "Is this a trick question?" "Is this relevant?" "Do I need to know all this?" "Would you please clarify?"

Procedures:

Step 1: Model the skill:

Using "Think Aloud" strategies—

1. Listen to what is said.

2. Ask my question in a friendly way.

3. Remember to say, "Thank you."

   Helpful Hints: Sometimes when we have questions, we don't wait until the speaker is done. If we ask a question too early, we often are embarrassed.

Step 2: Role play with feedback:

A. Have your students role play asking questions about a TV show or recent event. Ask each other if it was appropriate.

B. Have them ask questions about current events. Then answer the question—were they good listeners?

   Helpful Hints: Thought for this skill is: Good listeners have good questions. Ask a question in a rude way and see what the response is. Discuss. Do you deserve an answer?

Step 3: Transfer training:

A. **School:** Ask questions appropriately in P.E., music, or computer.

B. **Home/Community:** Ask questions about current events at the supper table.

C. **Peers:** Ask a friend a question about his or her life or family. Do you really know everything about your friend or do you just think you do?

Comments: Sometimes you ask people to clarify what you just heard. That is being a good listener when you do this because you want to make sure your interpretation is correct.

Extended Activities: Have a contest in the class for the day. Reward a person for asking a question appropriately. They are often the best listeners. Students who raise their hands a lot are not always the best listeners. Assign cooperative groups a subject to research and develop one good question on that subject to share with the class.

Lesson 13: Asking a Question

1. Listen to what is said.

2. Ask my question in a friendly way.

3. Remember to say, "Thank you!"

FRIENDSHIP SKILLS

Lesson 14: Appropriate Manners— Saying "Please" and "Thank You"

Objective: Students will be able to say "thank you" after receiving a compliment, present, or favor and "please" when asking for something.

Materials Needed: None.

Establish the Need: Set up a situation where you really need help. Use "please" and "thank you" to model. Read the stories, "Good Manners Work" and "The Lion and the Mouse," on the next page.

Procedures:

Step 1: Model the skill:

Using "Think Aloud" strategies—

1. What do I want?
2. Is it a good time to ask?
3. Say "Please, will you...?"
4. Thank the person.

Step 2: Role play with feedback:

A. Have your students pair off using "please" and "thank you" for different situations. Use good eye contact. Feedback.

B. Have your students practice "please" and "thank you" when it is appropriate in a school setting. Feedback.

Helpful Hints: What happens when we don't say "please" and "thank you?" Do people like you when you display poor manners? Discuss. Discuss what to do when someone refuses our request.

Step 3: Transfer training:

A. **School:** Practice using "please" and "thank you" on the playground and in the lunch room.

B. **Home/Community:** Practice good manners at home at the dinner table.

C. **Peers:** After someone has helped you, reward that person with praise and say, "Thank you, I appreciate it."

Comments: Some students think they don't need good manners away from adults, but respecting their peers requires the same behaviors and is a basis for friendship.

Extended Activities: Make a list of alternative words for "please" and "thank you."

Please	Thank you
Could you help me?	I appreciate that
I need your assistance.	Thanks
	No problem!

Good Manners Work!

Joy, one of the smaller girls in the fourth grade class, was always happy and go-lucky. Most of the time she prided herself as a very independent person who could do most anything by herself without help. One day, before a very important test, she misplaced her book. She needed to ask someone to use a book that night to study. She was reluctant to ask because when somebody else needed a favor she was very critical of that person's mistakes. She decided to ask another girl in class, but she turned her down. In fact, she asked three other girls and they did the same. Finally, she asked another girl, but this time she was very honest, "Please don't turn me down. I need to study very much." Using the word "please" helped her because the girl knew she was desperate and sincere. The girl agreed and from then on, Joy was more sympathetic to others and knew using good manners was the correct way to ask for favors. She was sure to "thank" her when she returned the book.

The Lion and the Mouse

The lion was asleep in his den one day when a mischievous mouse, for no reason at all, ran across the outstretched paw and up the royal nose of the king of beasts, awakening him from his nap. The mighty beast clapped his paw upon the mouse, thoroughly frightening the little creature. He could have made an end of him.

"Please," squealed the mouse, "don't' kill me. Forgive me this time, O King, and I shall never forget it. A day may come, who knows, when I may do you a good turn to repay your kindness." The lion, smiling at his little prisoner's fright and amused by the thought that so small a creature ever could be of assistance to the king of beasts, let him go.

Not long afterward, the lion, while stalking the forest for his prey, was caught in the net which the hunters had set to catch him. He let out a roar that echoed throughout the forest. Even the mouse heard it, and recognizing the voice of his former pursuer and friend, ran to the spot where he lay tangled in the net of ropes.

"Well your Majesty," said the mouse, "I know you did not believe me once when I said I would return a kindness, but here is my chance." And without further ado, he set to work to nibble with his sharp little teeth at the ropes that bound the lion. Soon the lion was able to crawl out of the hunter's snare to freedom. He was very grateful and said, "Thank you."

Application: No act of kindness, no matter how small, is ever wasted, and you will more likely receive help if you ask with good manners.

Lesson 14: Appropriate Manners: Saying "Please" and "Thank You"

1. What do I want?

2. Is it a good time to ask?

3. Say "Please, will you...?"

4. Thank the person.

FRIENDSHIP SKILLS

Lesson 15: Introducing Others

Objective: Students will be able to introduce others appropriately.

Materials Needed: None.

Establish the Need: Read the story, "Making Introductions," on the next page and discuss.

Procedures:

Step 1: Model the skill:

Use "Think Aloud" strategies while modeling the skills.

1. Name the first person—I would like you to meet (the name of the second person).
2. Name the second person and tell him or her the name of the first person.
3. Try to involve both people in a conversation.

Helpful Hints: It is also helpful to use both the first and last name. Use the name the person prefers. You can also identify each by principal, wife, father, and so forth.

Step 2: Role play with feedback:

A. Have your students divide into groups of three and take turns introducing each other and carrying on conversations. Rotate and give feedback.

B. Once they know how to introduce, keeping the conversation going is a more difficult task. Rotate and practice. Give feedback.

Helpful Hints: Help start a conversation by mentioning something or someone they both have in common. What happens when you don't introduce people? How do they feel? Act this out with your students.

Step 3: Transfer training:

A. **School:** Introduce adults to students and vice versa.

B. **Home/Community:** Introduce family members to your friends.

C. **Peers:** Introduce your best friend to others he or she doesn't know in the neighborhood.

Comments: This is a lifelong skill that needs to be practiced and guided by adults. A rule of thumb for etiquette is to say the name of the older person or person deserving more respect first and introduce the other person to them.

Extended Activities: Introduce speakers to the class or school staff. Have grandparents' day and have your students practice introducing their grandparents. Have your students introduce a fellow student as if he or she were

new.

Making Introductions

A very famous astronaut, John Glenn, comes to your school for a visit. You happen to be the Student Council Vice President. You have to give him a tour of the school because the Student Council President is sick. Major anxiety! You spend the whole day introducing him to the staff and classmates. "Mr. Glenn, this is our principal Mr. Nice Guy. Mr. Nice Guy, this is the famous astronaut, Mr. Glenn." Gee! I'm so glad our teacher practiced these social skills in our class. I don't have to look like a real "gleebe" in front of my classmates.

1. It is important to introduce people who don't know each other. Why?

2. Is it important to remember people's names when you introduce them?

Lesson 15: Introducing Others

1. Name the first person—I would like you to meet (the name of the second person).

2. Name the second person and tell him or her the name of the first person.

3. Try to involve both people in a conversation.

FRIENDSHIP SKILLS

Lesson 16: Joining In a Group

Objective: Students will learn how to ask to join a group in an appropriate way.

Materials Needed: Poster board.

Establish the Need: Read the story, "Moving Can Be Fun!," on the next page and discuss, and/or have your students act out. TV show: "Group Pressure," also on the next page.

Procedures:

Step 1: Model the skill:

Everyone wants to be able to join a group and not feel left out. Use "Think Aloud" strategies—

1. Do I want to join the group?
2. How do I approach the group?
3. Choose a good time.
4. Ask if I can join.
5. Wait for an answer.

Helpful Hints: Sometimes when a person take risks, he or she may not succeed. Discuss. Ask to join a group when there is a break in the action, or before it starts. What can you do if the group refuses you? (Do something else, find another group to ask, wait and try again later.)

Step 2: Role play with feedback:

A. Have your students take turns asking different groups if they can join. Observe and give feedback.

B. Have your students practice being rejected and practice choices of what they could do next.

Helpful Hints: Should girls ask a boys' group to join in or vice versa? What happens when someone just "bugs" others to join a group? What should be done? Have your students role play being rejected by group and then discuss what would happen if they started a fight, threw rocks, or called names. Discuss.

Step 3: Transfer training:

A. **School:** Practice this on the playground and in the lunchroom.

B. **Home/Community:** Practice this after school or on the weekend with games that people can join or be left out.

C. **Peers:** Practice helping others join in. What happens when people are left out?

Comments: When someone is left out, it can be a strain on friendships. Discuss. Why do people leave out others in a game?

Extended Activities: Discuss: Why is it important to be the best? Should we leave people out of games because they are not as good as those in the group? List TV shows that give you examples of this, "Full House," "Roseanne," "Grace Under Fire." Draw posters showing someone joining a group using "Think Aloud" strategies.

Moving Can Be Fun!

Jeff just moved to Denver. He went to the park where he saw kids his age playing soccer. He loved soccer! He didn't know anyone, and he was afraid to ask if he could join. He watched awhile. Finally, he asked a boy running by if he could join.

1. What would probably happen if Jeff didn't ask?
2. What might Jeff do if the boy says "no?"

TV Show: "Group Pressure"

TV show—characters: (need six)

1. John—Shy student—fair football player wants to join the group.
2. Five boys in a football game: Butch, Leroy, Harry, Ace, and Tom.
3. One leader in group—not a nice boy (Butch).
4. One boy in group—social worker, peace keeper (Tom).

You need six boys to act out this TV show. Have them make up their own lines. John is going to try to join the group. Butch doesn't want him to join. Tom thinks he should. What happens next? Give the group ten minutes to prepare the skit.

Lesson 16: Joining In a Group

1. Do I want to join the group?

2. How do I approach the group?

3. Choose a good time.

4. Ask if I can join.

5. Wait for an answer.

FRIENDSHIP SKILLS

son 17: Apologizing

Objective: Students will be able to apologize in a sincere manner for doing something wrong.

Materials Needed: Blackboard.

Establish the Need: First discuss what an apology is: TV shows have apologies on every night of the week. It seems easier on TV, but it is more difficult. Give examples and write on the board scenarios requiring an apology. (Lost or broke something, hurt someone's feelings, etc.)

Procedures:

Step 1: Model the skill:

Using "Think Aloud" strategies, establish a scenario: You lose paper a student handed in.

1. Did I do something wrong?
2. How should I apologize?
   a. Say, "I am sorry."
   b. Replace the object I lost or broke.
   c. Write them a note.
3. When is the best time and place to apologize?
   a. As soon as possible.
   b. In private.
4. Try to make amends.

Helpful Hints: Admitting you're wrong is the first step. You will actually feel better if you say you're sorry rather than ignore it. What does making amends mean?

Step 2: Role play with feedback:

Have your students pair up and practice apologizing and also receiving an apology in a gracious manner.

Helpful Hints: People will always make mistakes or break something. Apologize and go on with life. Discuss not apologizing and what might happen. Making amends is an important element.

Step 3: Transfer training:

A. **School:** Apologize to a teacher for not trying hard enough.

B. **Home/Community:** Apologize for something you did to a family member.

C. **Peers:** You could apologize for not being the best friend you can be.

Comments: Some people can easily say they are sorry, but they do nothing to rectify their error. Making amends is the final step in apologizing.

Extended Activities: Does a teacher ever apologize to a student? Be a model in your class for apologizing appropriately. Create a group of role play scenarios using "apologizing" to be presented to a younger class. Apologizing doesn't always mean you were wrong—it means you're sorry. Discuss the issue, "Being honest, but kind to your friend."

Lesson 17: Apologizing

1. Did I do something wrong?

2. How should I apologize?

   a. Say, "I am sorry."

   b. Replace the object I lost or broke.

   c. Write them a note.

3. When is the best time and place to apologize?

   a. As soon as possible.

   b. In private.

4. Try to make "amends."

FRIENDSHIP SKILLS

Lesson 18: Responding to Teasing

Objective: Students will ignore or change the subject when they are teased.

Materials Needed: None.

Establish the Need: Teasing can be both positive and negative. Friends can sometimes tease each other and laugh it off. But, teasing can be very harmful, especially if it involves name calling, making fun of other's looks. Discuss each. See the next page for a problem scenario. If both people are enjoying the teasing, it is probably okay.

Procedures:

Step 1: Model the skill:

Using "Think Aloud" strategies—

1. Decide if I am being teased.
2. Choices:
   a. Ignore.
   b. Walk away.
   c. Change the subject.

Helpful Hints: Why do people tease? (Gain attention, get a reaction.) Help your students see that teasing is fun for the "teaser" if the one being teased reacts.

Step 2: Role play with feedback:

A. Have your students pair up and role play responding to teasing using "Think Aloud" strategies.

Helpful Hints: Role play inappropriate responses to teasing: call them names back, fight, and argue. Should you respond this way? Discuss.

Step 3: Transfer training:

A. **School:** When others tease you on the playground, have a plan how you will respond.

B. **Home/Community:** Have your students talk about if they tease or are teased at home.

C. **Peers:** What can you do when you are teased by peers and you don't like it?

Comments: You have to know someone very well before you can tease that person in a positive way. You should be careful not to hurt the other's feelings. Treat others as you would want to be treated. Discuss how people feel when teasing versus being teased.

Extended Activities: Make a list of good teasing and bad teasing. Discuss name calling. Develop a list of scenarios in which teasing is harmful. Be sure to include disabilities, physical and cognitive features, and family issues. Discuss and help your students see that a "teaser" is dissatisfied and wants to put others down to feel better.

Calling People Names Can Be Harmful

Dear Know It All,

I'm fat and ugly. The other kids call me names. Nobody really likes me especially girls. I'm also a "klutz." Can you help me?

Tony

Dear Tony,

Who says you're fat and ugly? The people who are really important in your life, or a bunch of kids who want to make you mad? Believe me, Tony, you are not fat or ugly. Ugly doesn't have to do with your waist line or how big your ears are. It has to do with how you feel about yourself on the inside and how you treat others. Maybe the ones calling you names are the ones who have a problem.

Instead of concentrating on your faults or weaknesses, try finding out what you do well and what you like about yourself Try finding something you like to do that requires some sort of exercise and maybe you can lose weight at the same time. You may be surprised how much you like yourself once you start to concentrate on your strengths.

Know It All

1. How did Tony feel about the name calling?
2. What do you do when you are teased?

Lesson 18: Responding to Teasing

1. Decide if I am being teased.

2. Choices:

a. Ignore.

b. Walk away.

c. Change the subject.

FRIENDSHIP SKILLS

Lesson 19: Avoiding Inappropriate Physical Contact

Objective: Students will acknowledge and respect the boundaries of peers and adults.

Materials Needed: Large doll or stuffed animal, school counselor (optional).

Establish the Need: Discuss good touching and bad touching. When is physical contact appropriate? Inappropriate? See the story about Tom on the next page.

Procedures:

Step 1: Model the skill:

Using "Think Aloud" strategies—

1. Is the touching inappropriate or bad touching?
2. Choices:
   a. Walk away.
   b. Tell an adult.
   c. Tell the person, "I don't like it when you touch me."

Helpful Hints: Use a mannequin or large doll to model appropriate or inappropriate physical contact. *Do not model inappropriate physical contact with a live subject.* Counselors are very well trained in this. It is important to include being in someone else's space as well as the more intrusive kind of touching.

Step 2: Role play with feedback:

A. Have your students discuss when students hit or touch them. How do they feel? Role play. Feedback.

B. Discuss bad touching in large group. Discuss "respect" of others' boundaries.

Helpful Hints: List appropriate ways to gain the attention of others: tap on a shoulder, say the person's name. Model inappropriate touching. Discuss.

Step 3: Transfer training:

A. **School:** Make contact with someone in school by tapping on a shoulder to gain attention.

B. **Home/Community:** Appreciate your parents by a hug.

C. **Peers:** Give a friend a pat on the back for something well done.

Comments: Help your students see that we should not touch anyone else without the person's permission.

Extended Activities: Make a list of appropriate touching (hugging relatives, football, wrestling, dancing, handshakes). Refrain from: (1) hugging, (2) hand holding, and (3) touching anyone without permission.

Being Too Friendly

Tom was a good friend of everyone he knew. He had lots of friends. He was always polite, said nice things to his friends, shared his toys, and played fairly during class games. Although the other kids liked Tom most of the time, they were beginning to like him less and less. Tom had the habit of being too friendly. He was forever putting his arm around the shoulder of the other students, pinching their cheeks, patting them on the back, and hugging people when he was real happy. Tom thought he was being nice, but the kids didn't like being touched so often. After awhile, they started to run away from him, and soon they began to say mean things to him so he wouldn't touch them.

1. What could the kids have done instead of running away?

2. Should Tom's parents be told of this problem? Do they already know?

Lesson 19: Avoiding Inappropriate Physical Contact

1. Is the touching inappropriate or bad touching?

2. Choices:

a. Walk away.

b. Tell an adult.

c. Tell the person, "I don't like it when you touch me."

FRIENDSHIP SKILLS

Lesson 20: Listening to Your Peers

Objective: Students will listen when peers speak in class and in play situations.

Materials Needed: None.

Establish the Need: How long will you have friends, if you don't listen? See the next page for the story, "Please Listen, John."

Procedures:

Step 1: Model the skill:

Using "Think Aloud" strategies, model the following—

1. Make eye contact.
2. Continue occasional eye contact.
3. Give gestures or comments.

Helpful Hints: Peers need to have someone to listen to them. An essential quality of a friend is to listen.

Step 2: Role play with feedback:

A. Have your students pair up and practice listening to each other. Rotate and give feedback.

B. Have them practice not only listening, but keeping the conversation going using "Think Aloud" strategies.

Helpful Hints: Use starting and ending conversation techniques in this skill. Have your students ignore and not listen for contrast. Role play. Discuss.

Step 3: Transfer training:

A. **School:** Listen to peers on the playground. Did you remember what they said?

B. **Home/Community:** Listen to the conversation at meal time with friends. Report back to class on rules of a game that you made up during recess.

C. **Peers:** Listen to your best friend when he or she needs help without giving advice, just be a good listener.

Comments: This is a lifelong skill and needs practice and patience. This would be a good time to discuss Attention Deficit Disorder, a disorder that prevents some people from listening for a long period of time.

Extended Activities: Why do some children not listen to others'? Is it a lack of respect? Ask children why they listen to some children and not to others. Looks, height, respect, sex, smart, age, athletic—what is the reason? Draw a picture of how you feel when listened to. Divide class into 3s. Have one listener, one talker, and one observer for three minutes. The talker tells about his or her favorite activities. The listener says nothing, only listens. The observer sees how well person listens and gives feedback. See the next page. Also discuss that people who talk too much are not good listeners.

Friendship Skills

Please Listen, John

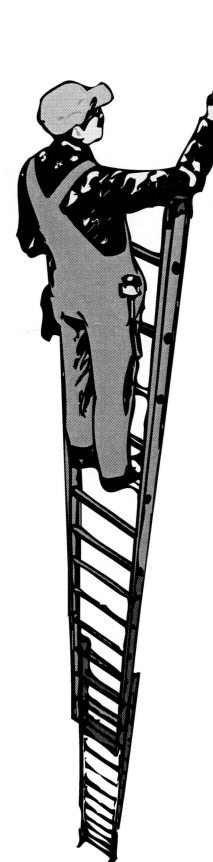

John was one of the worst day dreamers you could ever meet. When someone was talking about going out for pizza, John was thinking about baseball. When his friends told John to do something, he always did it wrong because he never seemed to listen. His parents, teacher, and friends were always saying, "Please listen, John." Sometimes he did and sometimes he didn't.

One day John and his friend, Jacob, were walking down the street near some stores. Jacob saw that a man was on a ladder painting one of the store signs. Jacob started talking about the man on the ladder and warned that they shouldn't get too close. Well, John never listened to what Jacob had to say. Because he did not listen to Jacob's warning, he bumped into the ladder and the man spilled a whole can of red paint all over John.

You might think that John would have learned to listen after the paint accident, but he hasn't. People are still saying, "Please listen, John."

Comments a Good Listener Can Say

1. You can say a brief encourager.

   great

   neat

   cool

   really?

   terrific

2. You can ask the person a question to show you'd like to know more about things.

   Then what happened?

   How did you do that?

   Where did you go next?

3. You can summarize what the person is saying.

   So what you're saying is....

   In other words, you....

   So you believe that....

Lesson 20: Listening to Your Peers

1. Make eye contact.

2. Continue occasional eye contact.

3. Give gestures or comments.

FRIENDSHIP SKILLS

Lesson 21: Tattling

Objective: Students will be able to recognize what tattling is and try to avoid doing it.

Materials Needed: Dictionary—look up "tattling"

Establish the Need: Read the story, "Honesty is the Best Policy," on the next page. Talk about the story, "Cry Wolf." Elicit from your students examples of problems which they handle themselves.

Procedures:

Step 1: Model the skill:

Using "Think Aloud" strategies, model handling tattling—

1. Is the problem major or minor?
2. Make a choice.
   a. Ignore.
   b. Say something.
   c. Major problem, tell an adult.
   d. Minor problem, handle it myself.

Helpful Hints: Ask your students to define tattling. A student should try to solve problem before telling an adult. Discuss examples of major and minor problems. How is tattling like gossip?

Step 2: Role play with feedback:

A. Role play appropriate ways to tell an adult when there is a major problem. Pair up. One person plays an adult. Rotate and make suggestions.

B. Switch roles and role play handling minor problems myself.

Helpful Hints: Telling the teacher or an adult about what another child did may not be the solution. Role play tattling. Discuss.

Step 3: Transfer training:

A. **School:** When something happens on the playground, practice trying to handle it yourself or talk about what to do instead of tattling.

B. **Home/Community:** If something happens in your neighborhood, discuss when police should be called or an adult notified.

C. **Peers:** When your friend does something wrong, should you tell someone or confront your friend?

Comments: Practice making good decisions. When you tell something that happens to an adult, you might lose respect of your peers. It is crucial that students can distinguish major problems and know who they need to tell.

Extended Activities: Tattling can be very annoying to adults, especially if the same person does it all the time. Children lose respect for those students. Tattling can be a serious problem and children need to know this. Create plays where students distinguish between minor and major problems and take appropriate action. Being a good friend means keeping appropriate secrets and promises. Discuss.

Honesty is the Best Policy

Rita was a fifth grade student who most people liked. She had one annoying problem. She tattled on everyone in the class, especially boys. One day she accidentally broke a school window. It was an accident, but she didn't tell any adult in school. Instead, she tried to ignore it because she knew she would get in trouble. However, the next day all the boys told on her. She got into double trouble because she wasn't honest. Her parents were also very upset. Rita learned a very good lesson. She should have told an adult herself. She finally realized what it felt like to be on the other side of the tattling.

1. Was this a major or minor problem?
2. How could Rita have handled the accident differently?

Lesson 21: Tattling

1. Is the problem major or minor?

2. Make a choice.

   a. Ignore.

   b. Say something.

   c. Major problem, tell an adult.

   d. Minor problem, handle it myself.

FRIENDSHIP SKILLS

Lesson 22: Sharing, Asking, and Giving

Objective: Students will be able to share personal items as well as school items without fighting and arguing.

Materials Needed: None.

Establish the Need: Read the stories, "Helping Others" and "Group Sharing," on the next page.

Procedures:

Step 1: Model the skill:

A. Model with a student using "Think Aloud" strategies on asking—

1. Should I ask?
2. Say, "Please can I share?"
3. "Thank you," if the answer is yes.
4. If the answer is no, what should I do?
   a. Ask another.
   b. Ask an adult.
   c. Go without.

B. Model with a student using "Think Aloud" strategies on giving:

1. Do I have plenty?
2. Do others have enough?
3. Should I offer to share?

Helpful Hints: Sharing is a lifelong skill. Some people never share. How do others view them? Stingy or selfish?

Step 2: Role play with feedback:

A. Divide in pairs. Switch by role playing both giving and asking.

B. Devise an activity for the next class where you have to share materials. Discuss what behavior you expect of your students.

Helpful Hints: What happens when people don't share or you ask someone to share and he or she tells you "no?" Discuss. Role play with feedback.

Step 3: Transfer training:

A. **School:** Set up activities in small groups where you have to share materials to complete work, art, and so forth.

B. **Home/Community:** Share a basketball or bike with your friends.

C. **Peers:** Share a treat with a friend.

Comments: It is very hard to ask people to share things, especially when you don't have anything to share back. What does "stingy" mean? Discuss.

Extended Activities: You share many things in this life. You share with friends, you share with family and students. How do you feel when you share or when you don't? Make a list of people with whom you share within a course of a week. Draw a picture of what family life would be like if members did not share.

Helping Others

The fifth grade class was going on a field trip to the dinosaur museum. Andy's mother was in the hospital, and he really wasn't himself this week so he forgot to bring his sack lunch. When the class stopped in the park to eat their lunches, Andy was feeling hungry. He noticed Brandon had a large lunch with two sandwiches. Working up his courage, he asked Brandon if he could have part of his lunch. Brandon said, "Sure, there's plenty here." They ate lunch and spent the rest of the day together.

Group Sharing

The fourth grade had an art project. Part of the project was to share colors, scissors, and paper. The class was divided into groups of four. The project was for sharing and cooperative learning. One group wasted the entire hour one day arguing and not sharing. The teacher decided to keep the group after school to work it out. It didn't take long for the group to finish.

1. What was the motivation to finish after school?
2. Is this a good project for fourth graders?

Lesson 22: Sharing, Asking, and Giving

A. Asking
1. Should I ask?
2. Say, "Please can I share?"
3. "Thank you," if the answer is yes.
4. If the answer is no, what should I do?
   a. Ask another.
   b. Ask an adult.
   c. Go without.

B. Giving
1. Do I have plenty?
2. Do others have enough?
3. Should I offer to share?

FRIENDSHIP SKILLS

Lesson 23: Respecting Others' Property

Objective: Students will be able to recognize others' property and respect their rights.

Materials Needed: None.

Establish the Need: Talk about this statement, "Treat others' property as you would treat your own." Discuss. Why do people destroy others' and public property? What are the consequences of this destruction?

Procedures:

Step 1: Model the skill:

Model using "Think Aloud" strategies—

1. Whose property is this?
2. If it is not mine, I should treat it like it was mine.
3. If I should damage it—replace it.
4. If I find something that is valuable—I should try to find the owner.

Helpful Hints: If you borrow someone's property, the owner would like it returned in the same shape or value. What does respect mean? Discuss.

Step 2: Role play with feedback:

A. Role play with students on how to respect others' property or school property. Role play with apologizing and repayment. Discuss

B. Role play destroying (scenario) of public property. Should you be held accountable? Discuss.

Helpful Hints: You borrow something from another student and you break it, but blame it on others or it was already broken. Discuss.

Step 3: Transfer training:

A. **School:** Ask to borrow a pencil, but when you ask say, "please" and say, "I will return it when I am done."

B. **Home/Community:** Should you respect the home you live in? Your parents' property?

C. **Peers:** Ask your friend how you should respect his or her property.

Comments: Destroying others' property is a serious problem and can lead to crimes later in life. Discuss vandalism.

Extended Activities: Discuss criminal charges against damaging property. Have you ever gotten in trouble from your teacher or neighbor for destroying or damaging property or possessions (trampling flowers, breaking windows)? Should you admit it and take your punishment, or should you hide and pretend you didn't do it? What could the class do to eliminate vandalism? Brainstorm. Perhaps take on a class project to decrease vandalism.

Dennis Hanken, Ed.S. and Judith Kennedy, Ed.S.

Lesson 23: Respecting Others' Property

1. Whose property is this?

2. If it is not mine, I should treat it like it was mine.

3. If I should damage it— replace it.

4. If I find something that is valuable—I should try to find the owner.

FRIENDSHIP SKILLS

Lesson 24: Dealing with "Cliques"

Objective: Students will be able to be friends with others without starting "cliques" and ignoring others.

Materials Needed: Blackboard, paper ,and pencil.

Establish the Need: Define "clique": Two or more students who don't want any more members and ignore others. They may be mean to others and act like a gang. Your students should make a secret list of who are the "cliques" in each room and discuss how new students and outsiders feel. Why do people gang together to ignore others? Talk about being "popular." Read the story, "Are You Popular?" on the following page.

Procedures:

Step 1: Model the skill:

Using "Think Aloud" strategies—

1. Is this a clique?
2. Am I being left out?
3. Am I leaving out someone else?
4. What is a good choice?

Helpful Hints: Can "cliques" be a positive influence? Yes, if they don't make fun of others and are open to others joining.

Step 2: Role play with feedback:

A. Role play with students having a group of friends, but not excluding and hurting others. Sports team, Girl Scouts, anyone can join.

B. Have your students practice inviting new people to play.

Helpful Hints: "Cliques" can be very hurtful and powerful. Have your students role play a bad "clique" and how it affects others. Discuss.

Step 3: Transfer training:

A. **School:** You hang around with three other girls. Another girl likes one of the three girls. You all decide to let her hang out with you. Is this a "clique?" Discuss.

B. **Home/Community:** Ask others to join in your neighborhood games even though you may not like them.

C. **Peers:** Ask another student to join in a game or activity even though he or she is not a close friend.

Comments: Discuss what peer pressure is. Good friends encourage other friendships.

Extended Activities: List examples of good "cliques" that have positive influences and a list of bad "cliques" that have negative influence.

GOOD	BAD
Scouts	Gangs
Sports teams	Groups joined by a common hatred

Are You Popular?

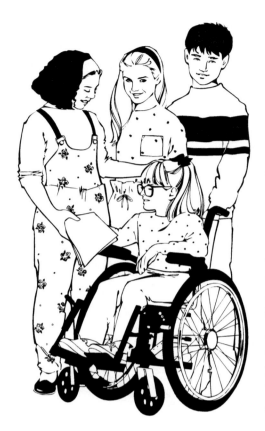

Three girls' attitudes about "cliques":

Debbie describes herself as being "one of the most popular girls in a not-very-popular group." I'm not part of the "in" crowd, but among my set of friends, I'm well liked. I'm not impressed by the popular crowd, either. I think a lot of them are stuck up and that they're often mean to other unpopular kids. "If that's what it takes to be popular, I'd rather just skip it" is my attitude.

Tanya is part of the most popular group at school, but she doesn't always feel real great about her popularity. Sometimes she's afraid to do or say certain things because she's afraid she'll lose "popularity points." She's afraid that other people won't like her anymore unless she acts a certain way.

Kristine feels like a tagalong. She's sort of on the edges of the popular group, but she's not really "in." She sometimes feels that the other girls would just as soon not have her around. She'd give anything to be more accepted and more popular. She often feels depressed or hurt because she's not popular.

Discuss these three girls and how they are different and what their role is in "cliques."

12 Ways to Make and Keep Friends

1. Don't put others down.
2. Tell others what you like about them.
3. Make others feel special.
4. Be truthful.
5. Keep secrets and promises.
6. Be a good listener.
7. See your friend's point of view.
8. Encourage others when they try to do hard things.
9. Help others feel better when they make a mistake.
10. Apologize if you hurt someone's feelings.
11. Forgive others if they hurt your feelings.
12. Let your friends have other friends.

Lesson 24: Dealing With "Cliques"

1. Is this a clique?

2. Am I being left out?

3. Am I leaving out someone else?

4. What is a good choice?

FRIENDSHIP SKILLS

Dennis Hanken, Ed.S. and Judith Kennedy, Ed.S.

Lesson 25: Note Passing

Objective: Students will be able to recognize that note passing can hurt others' feelings, that it may not be private, and that the student may miss information while writing notes during class.

Materials Needed: None.

Establish the Need: Have a time set aside when students may write notes to their classmates. Remove the secrecy. See the exercises on the next page.

Procedures:

Step 1: Model the skill:

Using "Think Aloud" strategies—

1. Should I write the note?
2. Is this the time and place?
3. Can I say it another way?
   a. In person.
   b. On the phone.
   c. Wait until another time.

Helpful Hints: You may write a note that you think is harmless, but anybody could find the note and you could get into trouble.

Step 2: Role play with feedback:

A. Role play students writing positive notes at the right time (before and after school lunch). Discuss.

B. Role play students writing "thank you" notes or activity notes, but not during class time.

Helpful Hints: You write a note to another student saying bad things about your teacher. Your teacher reads it and calls your parents. Discuss.

Step 3: Transfer training:

A. **School:** Write a note to your teacher saying how much you like the way he or she helps you.

B. **Home/Community:** Write a note to your parents saying how much you love them.

C. **Peers:** Write a "thank you" note to your best friend saying how much you appreciate that friend.

Comments: Writing hurtful things can cause harm. Discuss missing important class information when writing notes during class.

Extended Activities: Make a list of when you should write notes and also what is appropriate to say in notes. You don't want to write anything bad about someone because it could always wind up in someone's hand who could misinterpret what you say. Set up a suggestion box in the class. Have specified times for writing notes.

Educational Media Corporation®, Box 21311, Minneapolis, MN 55421-0311

Mixed Messages

Tell a made-up story about two girls in a classroom. One student is mad at the other for talking to her friend or being too friendly. The girl wants the whole class to know about it. Have everyone in the class write a note the girl might have written and read the notes aloud. Some are nasty, some are funny, and some are dumb, but the story is not always the same.

Don't Write It If You Don't Mean It!

Jill writes a bad note to Amber saying that she hates the teacher and wishes she was dead. The teacher finds the note on the floor. The teacher calls Jill's parents.

1. What do you think happens next?
2. Should Jill apologize to her teacher and Amber?

Lesson 25: Note Passing

1. Should I write the note?

2. Is this the time and place?

3. Can I say it another way?

a. In person.

b. On the phone.

c. Wait until another time.

FRIENDSHIP SKILLS

Lesson 26: Expressing Sympathy

Objective: Students will express sympathy to someone who has been hurt or experienced a loss.

Materials Needed: None.

Establish the Need: Read this story: *"Becky and Susan were best friends. They had been friends since first grade. They played together after school and slept over at each other's houses. When they were in the fifth grade, Becky's family moved to Minneapolis. Susan was lost without Becky. She was very lonely."* Discuss: (a) How did Susan feel? What had she lost? (b) What could you do or say to Susan to help her feel better?

Procedures:

Step 1: Model the skill:

Model using "Think Aloud" strategies—expressing sympathy with a described scenario.

1. Does the person have a hurt or loss?
2. Do I think I can help?
3. What can I do?
4. Do it.

Helpful Hints: It is helpful to give students some ideas on what to say, i.e., "I'm sorry." "How can I help?"

Step 2: Role play with feedback:

A. In pairs, have your students take turns expressing sorrow over an upcoming move to another town, a lost coat, or a broken arm.

B. Role play where you first learned or witnessed someone expressing sympathy.

Helpful Hints: It is good to help your students recognize how they feel with a loss and what others could do to help them feel better. How does one feel when someone is ignored in these situations?

Step 3: Transfer training:

A. **School:** Alert other school personnel to the skill you are working on and ask them to reinforce expressing sympathy when appropriate.

B. **Home/Community:** Ask parents to reinforce expressing sympathy.

C. **Peers:** Role play various scenarios in pairs: (1) The student's mother is having surgery. (2) The student's bicycle is stolen. (3) The student has lost homework. (4) The student falls and gets hurt.

Comments: Even adults hold back rather than express sympathy for fear of saying the wrong thing. This skill is important for students to learn.

Extended Activities: (1) Students write notes of sympathy for appropriate loss of someone they know. (2) Draw pictures showing how they feel when they have had a significant loss. (3) Journal how others could help them feel better after they have had a loss. "Homework Form," page 14 and "Expressing My Feelings Award," page 80.

Lesson 26: Expressing Sympathy

1. Does the person have a hurt or loss?

2. Do I think I can help?

3. What can I do?

4. Do it.

EXPRESSING FEELINGS

Expressing
My Feelings Award
to

_____

for using the skill of

_____

Date _____

Signed_____

Dennis Hanken, Ed.S. and Judith Kennedy, Ed.S.

Lesson 27: Making Positive Statements

Objective: Students will make five positive self-statements.

Materials Needed: Drawing paper.

Establish the Need: Read the story: "Bob and Jim were in fifth grade. Bob bragged about everything he did. His parents were the richest, his bike was the best, he was the smartest. His classmates did not like him, but they really did not like Jim either. Jim always said, "I'm dumb," "I don't do anything right." (1) Is it possible to always be the best or the "coolest?" (2) Can you say things about yourself without bragging or putting yourself down?

Procedures:

Step 1: Model the skill:

Model using "Think Aloud" strategies making positive self-statements.

1. What can I do well?
2. What do I like about myself?

Helpful Hints: It is often hard for people to state their strengths realistically. It will help if you model this in the classroom.

Step 2: Role play with feedback:

A. In pairs, have your students take turns saying a positive thing about themselves.

B. Practice making positive statements that others say about you.

Helpful Hints: Journaling is a good, nonthreatening way for students to write positives about themselves. What do negatives do to a person's self-concept?

Step 3: Transfer training:

A. **School:** Ask the playground staff to ask students to tell them one good thing about themselves.

B. **Home/Community:** Write parents a note asking them to discuss with their children some of their good qualities.

C. **Peers:** Have your students write a note to a friend stating one good quality the friend has.

Comments: Students tend to hear many more negative than positive comments about themselves. For learning to be optimal they should hear *five* positive statements for every *one* negative. This is true for self-talk too.

Extended Activities: (1) Students make a drawing or collage of themselves depicting their good qualities. (2) Students make a list of five affirmations to say aloud to themselves every day in front of a mirror. "Homework Form," page 14 and "Expressing My Feelings Award," page 80.

Lesson 27: Making Positive
Self-Statements

1. What can I do well?

2. What do I like about myself?

EXPRESSING FEELINGS

Lesson 28: Knowing What You are Feeling

Objective: Students will become aware of the feelings they are having.

Materials Needed: "List of Feelings" page 85, journals.

Establish the Need: Go over the feelings in the "List of Feelings." Ask your students to depict by body and facial expression each feeling. Talk about physical sensations that accompany feelings (butterflies in stomach, tenseness, exhaustion, shaky, nausea, etc.).

Procedures:

Step 1: Model the skill:

Model using "Think Aloud" strategies, knowing what you are feeling—

  1. What is my body feeling?
  2. What caused me to feel this way?
  3. Label my feeling.

Helpful Hints: Some students will have been taught to not have feelings. It will be important to teach them that feelings are normal and healthy, but we do need to be thoughtful in how we express our feelings.

Step 2: Role play with feedback:

A. Have your students journal some feelings they have had, what their body told them, and what caused them to feel that way.

B. Role play how your body feels when you are mad, sad, happy, worried, and so forth.

Helpful Hints: For students who seem unable to label feelings, a referral to the school counselor might be considered. Many people don't recognize body signals for feelings. This may lead to stomachaches or headaches. Discuss.

Step 3: Transfer training:

A. **School:** Ask the playground personnel to reinforce students getting in touch with their feelings and labeling them.

B. **Home/Community:** Tell parents what skill you are working on, asking students to report one situation at home and what their feelings were.

C. **Peers:** Your best friend won't play with you at recess. How do you feel? What do you do? Discuss.

Comments: Your school counselor is an excellent resource for identifying feelings.

Extended Activities: (1) Stories or films depicting feelings and ways to deal with them. (2) Puppets help some children identify their feelings more easily. You could arrange a puppet show dealing with feelings. "Homework Form," page 14 and "Expressing My Feelings Award," page 80.

Lesson 28: Knowing What
You are Feeling

1. What is my body feeling?

2. What caused me to feel this way?

3. Label my feeling.

EXPRESSING FEELINGS

List of Feelings

Directions: Copy and cut out the list of feelings. In triads, have your students draw a card and demonstrate that feeling.

Mad	**Furious**
Happy	**Scared**
Sad	**Lonely**
Excited	**Upset**
Grouchy	**Frustrated**
Angry	**Nervous**
Worried	**Defeated**

Lesson 29: Showing Your Feelings

Objective: Students will choose how to express their feelings appropriately.

Materials Needed: List of feelings written on the board or a poster (happy, sad, mad, angry, nervous, frustrated, upset, lonely, worried, scared, furious, excited, grouchy).

Establish the Need: Read the stories, "Anger—Learn to Control It" and "Accepting Responsibilities for Actions," on the following page.

Procedures:

Step 1: Model the skill:

Model using "Think Aloud" strategies—expressing your feelings about going to a dentist or speaking at an important event.

1. What is my body feeling?
2. What caused me to feel this way?
3. Label my feelings.
4. What are my choices for ways to express my feeling?
5. Choose one.

Helpful Hints: Explore lots of options with your students on choices for expressing their feelings.

Step 2: Role play with feedback:

A. Create hypothetical scenarios which elicit feelings, i.e., no school tomorrow, you have to walk home alone by big dog, you are going on a trip, you get in trouble at school, you get picked for a team, your best friend is moving away, you are being teased).

B. Expressing feelings appropriately is better than acting out inappropriately. Discuss and role play.

Helpful Hints: Help your students discriminate between appropriate expression of feelings (walk away, talk feelings out to someone, exercise, express feelings) and inappropriate (fighting, hitting, keeping feelings inside).

Step 3: Transfer training:

A. **School:** You miss the ball when you are up to bat for the last time and your team was counting on you. How do you feel? How do you express feelings?

B. **Home/Community:** Your parents won't let you go to a show everyone else is seeing. How do you feel? How do you express feelings?

C. **Peers:** You do not get invited to a birthday party that your friends are attending. How do you feel? How do you express it?

Comments: Many adults have trouble expressing their feelings appropriately, so children may not have had much appropriate modeling. Be a good model and teach your students that appropriate expression of feelings is essential for good mental health.

Extended Activities: (1) Draw pictures or journal showing ways to express feelings appropriately. (2) There are many books and films on expressing feelings which could be used to show appropriate and inappropriate ways to express feelings and could facilitate discussion. "Homework Form," page 14 and "Expressing My Feelings Award," page 80.

Anger—Learn to Control It

Sarah was a girl who would throw things, slam doors, and scream when she was angry. Her parents were concerned that she made such poor choices for expressing her anger. One day Sarah was angry because she wanted to go swimming and her parents said she had to do her chores first. She picked up the camcorder and threw it.

1. What is Sarah feeling?
2. What are some ways you can express anger?
3. What would have been some better choices for Sarah?

Accepting Responsibility for Actions

Whenever John didn't get his way, he would pout for hours. Usually people would give into John and then he would continue doing this behavior. One day his teacher said he had to stay after school for talking during a test. John pouted for hours after this, thinking the teacher would change her mind. She didn't and he was furious. This happened many times, but John couldn't figure out why he couldn't change his teacher.

1. Do you think John will ever change his behavior?
2. Do you think his teacher will change her mind about keeping John after school?

Lesson 29: Expressing Your Feelings

1. What is my body feeling?

2. What caused me to feel this way?

3. Label my feelings.

4. What are my choices for ways to express my feeling?

5. Choose one.

EXPRESSING FEELINGS

Lesson 30: Understanding the Feelings of Others

Objective: Students will label feelings of others by observing facial expressions and body language.

Materials Needed: Pictures showing people expressing various feelings.

Establish the Need: Read this story: *"Beth was not invited to a birthday party that all of her friends were attending. She withdrew, wouldn't play with others at recess, and sulked. Her friends did not know she hadn't been invited or why she was acting this way."* (1) What is Beth feeling? (2) How can you tell? (3) What could her friends do to help her feel better?

Procedures:

Step 1: Model the skill:

Model understanding the feelings of others using "Think Aloud" strategies. Have another adult role play the feelings.

1. Watch the person.
2. Label the feeling.
3. Choose what I will do:
   a. Offer comfort.
   b. Ask why he or she is feeling that way.
   c. Leave the person alone.

Helpful Hints: Students need to recognize feelings and also choose their response to the person's feelings. Brainstorm options.

Step 2: Role play with feedback:

A. Pair students and have them take turns depicting a feeling by facial expression and body posture with the other one labeling the feeling.

B. Using the suggested sentences on the next page, have your students read a sentence with different voice inflections. Discuss.

Helpful Hints: For more practice you can clip photos from magazines or newspapers and have your students label the feelings in the photos.

Step 3: Transfer training:

A. **School:** Ask the school counselor to come and do an activity with your class on understanding others' feelings and choosing a response.

B. **Home/Community:** Ask the parents to discuss with their children how they know when their parents were angry, sad, or happy.

C. **Peers:** At recess, see one other child, label his or her feeling, decide on a response, and report back.

Comments: Some body responses are universal (butterflies in the stomach when you are afraid), while others are more individual. Brainstorm various body responses to feelings and role play them. Your tone of voice is important.

Extended Activities: (1) Create a play depicting major feelings (mad, happy, said, afraid). (2) Make a collage from magazines showing people with various feelings. Label those feelings. (3) Discuss how people in a nursing home might feel. How could respond to those feelings? Visit a nursing home. See the next page. "Homework Form," page 14 and "Expressing My Feelings Award," page 80.

Directions: for Role Play B, say these sentences with different inflections and tones to reflect anger, excitement, worry, sadness, fear, confusion, and relaxation. Then compare. Can you always tell them apart?

- I'm not doing anything.
- Your new friend is okay.
- Oh, that's just great.
- Are you sure she said that?
- I don't understand you.
- I am looking for it.
- Would you please do it?
- What are you doing?
- Oh, it was okay.

Is it easy to misinterpret others' feelings or misread what someone is saying?

How is the tone of voice a good clue to feelings?

Lesson 30: Understanding the Feelings of Others

1. Watch the person.

2. Label the feeling.

3. Choose what I will do:

a. Offer comfort.

b. Ask why he or she is feeling that way.

c. Leave the person alone.

EXPRESSING FEELINGS

Lesson 31: Sportsmanship

Objective: Students will learn how to lose and win appropriately.

Materials Needed: Card or board games.

Establish the Need: Read this story: *"Eric and Mary never get invited to play soccer. Eric doesn't get invited because he is not very good at playing soccer. Mary plays soccer well, but she doesn't get invited because she cries and calls people names if her team is losing. She also brags when her team wins and hogs the ball when she gets it."* (1) Why don't others pick Mary to play soccer? (2) What could Mary do for teammates to appreciate her more?

Procedures:

Step 1: Model the skill:

Model using "Think Aloud" strategies—showing good sportsmanship.

1. Follow the rules of the game.
2. Be courteous.
3. Give encouragement.
4. Keep playing until the game is over.
5. Congratulate the other team.

   Helpful Hints: Losing is hard for some children. Some techniques used in cooperative learning groups can be applied to sports as well.

Step 2: Role play with feedback:

A. In groups, students will role play losing a game using "Think Aloud" strategies.

B. In groups, students will role play winning a game using "Think Aloud" strategies.

   Helpful Hints: The other team should be congratulated on the game whether they win or not. Solicit ideas for congratulating, i.e., "good game," "nice game." Role play inappropriate gestures and name calling after losing a game. Discuss.

Step 3: Transfer training:

A. **School:** Ask the P.E. teacher to reinforce this skill while you are teaching it.

B. **Home/Community:** Play a board game with someone at home. Use good sportsmanship.

C. **Peers:** Accompany your students outside for an extra recess. Assign people to two teams to play kick ball, soccer, or softball. Practice sportsmanship.

Comments: Card games and academic games may also be used to practice this skill.

Extended Activities: (1) Periodically have students self-report on their progress of developing good sportsmanship. (2) You could arrange intramural sports events among the classes with a focus on good sportsmanship being practiced. "Handling Stress Award," page 94 and "Homework Form," page 14.

Lesson 31: Sportsmanship

1. Follow the rules of the game.

   a. No cheating.

   b. No fighting.

2. Be courteous.

3. Give encouragement.

4. Keep playing until the game is over.

5. Congratulate the other team.

"Congratulations: Good job!"

RELIEVING STRESS

Handling Stress Award

to

_____

for using the skill of

_____

Date _____

*Signed*_____

Lesson 32: Dealing with Fear—Relieving Stress

Objective: Students will label feeling of fear and make choice for dealing with fear.

Materials Needed: None.

Establish the Need: Read this story: *"Jody had to walk home from school by herself, and almost every day Bruce, a middle school student, would chase her and threaten to beat her up. Even if she changed her route, he seemed to find her."* (1) What is Jody feeling? (2) What action could she take to protect herself?

Procedures:

Step 1: Model the skill:

Establish the scenario of you being home alone at night late and someone knocks on the door. Model using "Think Aloud" strategies—dealing with fear:

1. What feelings are connected to fear?
2. What caused my fear?
3. I'm afraid.
4. Choose how to deal with the fear.

Helpful Hints: There are situations which are fearful for children and over which they have no power. Help them discriminate between the situations they can handle and the ones requiring assistance. Help them brainstorm possible actions for both situations.

Step 2: Role play with feedback:

A. Have your students journal about a situation which causes them fear. Have them list examples of possible action they could take.

B. Role play a fear you have about school. Discuss in small groups.

Helpful Hints: Some students may share a situation which is dangerous, i.e., abuse. It might be a good idea to have the school counselor help with this lesson. What happens when you let fear control you? Fear of dogs, darkness, water? Discuss.

Step 3: Transfer training:

A. **School:** Draw pictures of something at school that causes you fear.

B. **Home/Community:** Discuss with a trusted adult any situation which you can't handle that causes you fear.

C. **Peers:** Fred is the playground bully. Brainstorm possible actions you could take to avoid getting hurt.

Comments: Some children freeze when fearful and don't take any action. Help them to see what action they could take.

Extended Activities: (1) Ask the school counselor to do some class sessions on dealing with fear. (2) Brainstorm how fear can benefit us (protect us from danger, cause us to use caution, make us think about a situation, better understand others who are fearful of something). "Handling Stress Award," page 94 and "Homework Form," page 14.

Lesson 32: Dealing with Fear

1. What feelings are connected to fear?

2. What caused my fear?

3. I'm afraid.

4. Choose how to deal with the fear.

RELIEVING STRESS

Lesson 33: Handling Group Pressure

Objective: Students will recognize peer pressure and choose a response.

Materials Needed: None.

Establish the Need: Read this story: *"John, Sean, and Liz were shopping together. John wanted to steal a CD, and he wanted Liz to hide it in her coat pocket for him until they were out of the store. Liz really liked John and was afraid she would lose his friendship. Sean called her a chicken if she wouldn't do it."* (1) What does John want Liz to do? (2) What is Liz feeling? (3) What are some choices of action Liz could take?

Procedures:

Step 1: Model the skill:

Set the scenario of fellow teacher needing to leave school early and needing ride from you. Model using "Think Aloud" strategies—handling group pressure.

1. What do they want me to do?
2. Do I want to do it?
3. Say "no" or compromise!

Helpful Hints: It might be helpful to discuss other ways of dealing with pressure, the consequences of each: yield, resist, delay, avoid, say "no," compromise.

Step 2: Role play with feedback:

A. In groups of three, students will practice handling pressure. One student pressures, one handles it, one observes and gives feedback. Rotate roles.

B. Role play group pressure that is positive—group projects. Discuss.

Helpful Hints: Possible scenarios: Pressure to go somewhere your parents said no, pressure to vandalize, steal, smoke, cheat, fight with someone. What happens when you give in to the group and you really didn't want to? Discuss.

Step 3: Transfer training:

A. **School:** Your best friend wants to copy your math homework. What do you do?

B. **Home/Community:** A group of friends you are with want to throw rocks through the window of a troublesome neighbor. What do you do?

C. **Peers:** Several of your friends are ganging up on a classmate and want you to join in. What do you do?

Comments: Fourth and fifth graders have pressure to join cliques and exclude others. This is a good time to address this. Your school counselor might assist.

Extended Activities: (1) In groups, brainstorm possible events where you might get group pressure to go along. Brainstorm possible action. (2) Create a play where students are pressuring someone and the choices that person makes. "Handling Stress Award," page 94 and "Homework Form," page 14.

Lesson 33: Handling Group Pressure

1. What do they want me to do?

2. Do I want to do it?

3. Say "no" or compromise.

RELIEVING STRESS

Lesson 34: Stating a Complaint

Objective: Students will state a complaint to adults or peers.

Materials Needed: None.

Establish the Need: Read this story: *"Becky saved her baby-sitting money to buy a new shirt she had wanted for a long time. When she got the shirt home, the seam under the arm was open and frayed."* (1) What might Becky complain about? (2) What are some possible ways she could make the complaint?

Procedures:

Step 1: Model the skill:

Set the scenario: You need to use the copier before class and another teacher has been on it for 1/2 hour. Model using "Think Aloud" strategies—making a complaint:

1. What injustice have I suffered?
2. Decide who to complain to.
3. Stand up, use a strong voice.
4. Keep trying until I get an answer.

Helpful Hints: Your students also need to recognize the positive and negative consequences of making a complaint and proceed if they decide it is better to complain.

Step 2: Role play with feedback:

A. Brainstorm possible scenarios (boy won't share ball, teacher blames you for something you did not do, classmate accuses you of taking his pencil). Group students in 3s or 4s and have them alternate role playing.

B. Role play making a complaint to a parent or an adult about an unfair command.

Helpful Hints: It will be helpful to practice some specific words to use, i.e., "Excuse me, but that is my ball." "This shirt I bought has a hole in it." Role play a complaint that is ignored. Discuss.

Step 3: Transfer training:

A. **School:** Ask your lunchroom personnel to receive a complaint from your students.

B. **Home/Community:** Students will write a letter of complaint for a defective product to an improvised or real store.

C. **Peers:** Students are to make a complaint to a friend and report back.

Comments: It is often easier to complain to people one doesn't know than to friends. Explore with your students the reasons for this. Honor your students' rights for legitimate complaints in classroom.

Extended Activities: (1) Students can brainstorm a concern within the community and write a letter from the class expressing the complaint. (2) Help your students discuss the difference between making a complaint and tattling. Discuss (making a complaint occurs when we have suffered an injustice and go directly to the person who did it to have it corrected). "Handling Stress Award," page 94 and "Homework Form," page 14.

Lesson 34: Making a Complaint

1. What injustice have I suffered?

2. Decide who to complain to.

3. Stand up, use a strong voice.

4. Keep trying until I get an answer.

RELIEVING STRESS

Lesson 35: Responding to a Complaint

Objective: Students will listen to a complaint about self and respond politely.

Materials Needed: 3 x 5 cards that you prepared in advance containing various complaints.

Establish the Need: Read this story: *"Amber looked forward to eating the chocolate chip cookie in her lunch. When lunchtime came, her cookie was gone. She remembered Susan had been in her desk."* (1) What is Amber's complaint? (2) What might she say to Susan? (3) How might Susan respond?

Procedures:

Step 1: Model the skill:

Model using "Think Aloud" strategies—responding to a complaint that you wrongly accused a student of cheating.

1. Listen to the complaint.
2. Think before responding.
3. Ask questions.
4. Choose your response: a) Apologize. b) Compromise. c) Do nothing.

Helpful Hints: Students need to know that people will not always receive their complaints well. What are possible consequences of making a complaint? (Rejection, arguments, anger, blame.)

Step 2: Role play with feedback:

A. In groups of 3 or 4 students, role play answering a complaint written on the 3 x 5 cards.

B. Answer a complaint by a teacher for a late assignment or a poor grade.

Helpful Hints: Help students to recognize the difference between a complaint of injustice and criticism.

Step 3: Transfer training:

A. **School:** Ask other school personnel to make a complaint to your students to practice the skill.

B. **Home/Community:** Ask the parents to make a complaint to their children. Discuss in class.

C. **Peers:** Report to class how you handled a complaint from a friend.

Comments: Even adults get defensive in responding to complaints. Students can learn they have a right to stand up for themselves and to admit fault if it is true.

Extended Activities: (1) Arrange with other classroom teachers to make complaints to your students and to assist them to respond using "Think Aloud" strategies. (2) You can be a good model in responding to students' complaints. (3) This is a difficult skill and may need additional practice. Students can write skits depicting making and answering complaints. "Handling Stress Award," page 94 and "Homework Form," page 14.

Relieving Stress

Lesson 35: Answering a Complaint

1. Listen to the complaint.

2. Think before responding.

3. Ask questions.

4. Choose your response:

a. Apologize.

b. Compromise.

c. Do nothing.

RELIEVING STRESS

Lesson 36: Handling Embarrassment

Objective: Students will take action when they feel embarrassed.

Materials Needed: Humorous pictures showing people in embarrassing situations.

Establish the Need: Read this story: *"Jeff was reporting to class on his social studies project, a model of an early frontier fort. On the way to the front of the room he tripped over John's foot, fell and dropped his fort scattering it all over the floor."* (1) How does Jeff probably feel? (2) What could he do to feel less embarrassed? (3) Brainstorm situations in which a student might feel embarrassment. (4) Show pictures and discuss.

Procedures:

Step 1: Model the skill:

Model using "Think Aloud" strategies—handling embarrassment when you have spilled your food at a formal dinner.

1. Am I embarrassed?
2. What caused it?
3. What can I do?
4. Choose action: a) Ignore. b) Joke about it. c) Reassure myself. d) Admit what I did. e) Change the subject.

Helpful Hints: Sometimes if students use the "worst case" scenario, they are less embarrassed. That is, they imagine the worst possible thing that could happen in the situation.

Step 2: Role play with feedback:

A. Create embarrassing situations, write on the board. In pairs, have your students role play the scenarios.

B. Role play your most embarrassing moment and what you did. Discuss the results.

Helpful Hints: Possible scenarios: spilling food, spilling water on front of pants, dropping something, having clothing partly unfastened, saying something that others laugh at.

Step 3: Transfer training:

A. **School:** You are called on by your teacher to do a math problem at the board that you don't know how to do.

B. **Home/Community:** You answer the door with your siblings fighting and yelling and it is someone from church.

C. **Peers:** You spill your milk all over a friend at lunch. Everyone laughs.

Comments: Embarrassment is sometimes worse for children who blush because that can be the next embarrassment.

Extended Activities: (1) Journal about an embarrassing experience. (2) Draw an embarrassing scene and how you could handle it to be less embarrassed. "Handling Stress Award," page 94 and "Homework Form," page 14.

Relieving Stress

Lesson 36: Handling Embarrassment

1. Am I embarrassed?

2. What caused it?

3. What can I do?

4. Choose action:

a. Ignore.

b. Joke about it.

c. Reassure myself.

d. Admit what I did.

e. Change the subject.

RELIEVING STRESS

Dennis Hanken, Ed.S. and Judith Kennedy, Ed.S.

Lesson 37: What to do When You are Left Out

Objective: Students will list other options when feeling left out.

Materials Needed: None.

Establish the Need: Read this story: *"A group of girls were standing in the hall after school planning a going away party for Amy. Jo joined in the discussion and development of plans. As the talking progressed, Mary suggested they go to her house to finish planning. As they talked about rides and getting there, Jo was left out. She felt very bad as everyone else walked away excited."* Discuss.

Procedures:

Step 1: Model the skill:

Model using "Think Aloud" strategies—what to do when you are excluded from an activity.

1. Why am I feeling left out?
2. What can I do about it?
   a. Ask to join.
   b. Tell how I feel.
   c. Find something else to do.
3. Choose and do it.

Helpful Hints: Scenarios for exclusion: (1) only person not invited to party, (2) game, (3) talking, (4) playing.

Step 2: Role play with feedback:

A. In pairs, have your students practice using "Think Aloud" strategies—being left out. Give each other feedback.

B. You are left out of a birthday party. What do you do? Discuss

Helpful Hints: Rotate and give feedback. You are left out of a game during recess. You call everyone names. Discuss.

Step 3: Transfer training:

A. **School:** Ask the P.E. teacher to reinforce the students who use "Think Aloud" strategies for being left out.

B. **Home/Community:** Students report back on how they felt about being left out by someone in their neighborhood.

C. **Peers:** Journal how you would handle being left out of a birthday party.

Comments: Find something else to do is a choice of which students may be unaware.

Extended Activities: (1) Draw pictures of how they feel when left out and how they feel when they choose an action suggested in "Think Aloud." Write a sentence about how you feel when you are left out. "Handling Stress Award," page 94 and "Homework Form," page 14.

Lesson 37: What to Do When You are Left Out

1. Why am I feeling left out?

2. What can I do about it?

a. Ask to join.

b. Tell how I feel.

c. Find something else to do.

3. Choose and do it.

RELIEVING STRESS

Lesson 38: Defending a Friend

Objective: Students will stand up for a friend who is being treated unfairly.

Materials Needed: None.

Establish the Need: Read this story: *"Brad was small for sixth grade. He often got bumped in the halls or on the playground. Alfred was a big boy who liked to pick on people smaller than he. Whenever he saw Brad, he would trip him or shove him into something."* (1) If Brad were your friend, what could you do to help him? (2) Have you or a friend of yours ever been treated unfairly?

Procedures:

Step 1: Model the skill:

Model the skill using "Think Aloud" Strategies:

1. Decide if a friend is being treated unfairly.
2. Decide if a friend wants my help.
3. How can I help my friend?
   a. Tell an adult.
   b. Speak up.
4. Do it.

Helpful Hints: You may need to discuss unfair treatment, i.e., teasing, bullying, wrongly accused or punished.

Step 2: Role play with feedback:

A. Have your students role play using "Think Aloud" strategies in groups of three, rotating roles and providing feedback.

B. Defend an adult friend. Is this the same? Discuss and provide feedback.

Helpful Hints: It will be helpful to brainstorm possible scenarios and write them on the board. What happens when you don't defend your friend? Does this put a stress on your friendship?

Step 3: Transfer training:

A. **School:** Ask the playground personnel to set up instances where your students can practice standing up for a friend.

B. **Home/Community:** Stand up for a family member or friend in your neighborhood. Report back.

C. **Peers:** Look for opportunities to stand up for a friend. Report back.

Comments: This is a tough skill. Provide numerous opportunities to practice and reinforce.

Extended Activities: (1) Role play a student standing up for a friend who is being teased. (2) Have your students write as many ideas as they can for ways they could stand up for a friend. (3) Discuss famous people in history who stood up for other people (Martin Luther King, Ghandi, Mother Teresa, Albert Schweitzer) and how they did it. (4) Students write a brief report on a person of their choice who stood up for other people. "Handling Stress Award," page 94 and "Homework Form," page 14.

Relieving Stress

Lesson 38: Defending a Friend

1. Decide if a friend is being treated unfairly.

2. Decide if a friend wants my help.

3. How can I help my friend?

   a. Tell an adult.

   b. Speak up.

4. Do it.

RELIEVING STRESS

Lesson 39: Responding to Peer Pressure

Objective: Students will identify pressure and choose a way to respond.

Materials Needed: Film/video of choice on dealing with persuasion, i.e., drug and alcohol film.

Establish the Need: Read this story: *"Emily was supposed to go home right after school. A group of kids were going to go hang out at Rob's house since his parents were at work. Emily wanted to go too, and her friends encouraged her to lie to her parents and say she had a meeting after school."* (1) Have you ever been pressured to do something you knew you shouldn't? (2) What do you think Emily should do?

Procedures:

Step 1: Model the skill:

Model using "Think Aloud" strategies—responding to pressure to cheat on a test. Consequences of decisions.

1. Decide if I'm being pressured.
2. What could happen if I do this?
3. Decide what I want to do.
4. Do it.

Helpful Hints: Possible scenarios: stay out late, steal, spend money, drink alcohol, commit vandalism.

Step 2: Role play with feedback:

A. Role play in small groups responding to peer pressure using "Think Aloud" strategies.

B. You are pressured to cheat by several classmates. Discuss and rotate.

Helpful Hints: This will be really tough for the student who is a follower. It will help to brainstorm numerous options for responding to pressure.

Step 3: Transfer training:

A. **School:** Ask the counselor to come into class and practice other scenarios and their responses.

B. **Home/Community:** Friends are going to break into the swimming pool at night and swim. Discuss what you would do.

C. **Peers:** Your friend wants you to lie to his or her parent, and say they were staying over night at your house.

Comments: You can also connect this to withstanding sales pressure or unwanted physical attention.

Extended Activities: (1) Journal about ways someone is pressuring you, your feelings, and what you choose to do about it. (2) You could do this lesson as part of drug and alcohol awareness or harassment curriculum. "Handling Stress Award," page 94 and "Homework Form," page 14.

Relieving Stress

Lesson 39: Responding to Peer Pressure

1. Decide if I'm being pressured.

2. What could happen if I do this?

3. Decide what I want to do.

4. Do it.

RELIEVING STRESS

Lesson 40: Responding to Failure

Objective: Students will make positive choices in dealing with failure.

Materials Needed: Board games.

Establish the Need: Read this story: *"Emily was good at reading, but she never could get those long division problems. No matter how hard she tried, she couldn't remember the steps to do and keep all the numbers straight. She wondered if she should just copy off Tim's paper."* (1) What is Emily's response to failure? (2) What else could she choose?

Procedures:

Step 1: Model the skill:

Model using "Think Aloud" strategies—failing your driver's license test.

1. Did I fail?
2. Why did I fail?
3. What can I do to prevent failing next time?
4. What do I do now?

   a. Try again.

   b. Do something else.

   c. Ask for help.

Helpful Hints: Discuss whether it does any good to get angry when we fail.

Step 2: Role play with feedback:

A. In small groups, role play responding to failure using "Think Aloud" strategies.

B. Role play failing a test. Rotate and discuss.

Helpful Hints: Possible scenarios: failing a test, failing to keep a friendship, failing at a sport, game, or music lesson. After you fail a test, you just give up the rest of the year. Discuss.

Step 3: Transfer training:

A. **School:** Ask the P.E. teacher to reinforce this lesson in activities this week.

B. **Home/Community:** What is something you have tried at home and failed (whistling, cart wheels, Nintendo, a sport)? Discuss.

C. **Peers:** How do you feel when you fail at something your friend is good at. Journal.

Comments: We all fail at something. Bring that out in the discussion. Also, suggest ways we can learn from our failure. Does luck ever come into play in failure? Motivation?

Extended Activities: (1) Share Ten Tips to Taking a Test on the next page. (2) Brainstorm ideas for avoiding failure. (3) Write about the difference in failing at a task and being a failure as a person. "Handling Stress Award," page 94 and "Homework Form," page 14.

Relieving Stress

Tips for Doing Well on Tests

1. Go to bed on time the night before and get up in time for a good breakfast.

2. Be sure you have all the materials you need—a sharpened pencil, paper, books, notes, maps. Whatever you need.

3. Read the directions before starting the test. If you don't understand something, ask your teacher.

4. Answer all the questions you know first, leaving the ones you are uncertain of until later. However, it is usually best not to go back and change answers, as your first response is often correct.

5. Be sure that your answer every question.

6. Stay relaxed. If you mind wanders or you feel anxious, breathe deeply.

7. Check the clock periodically to make sure you will have enough time to complete the test. Don't hurry. Use the time you need.

8. Check your finished paper before handing it in to make sure you answered every item.

9. Study a little each day prior to the test, instead of waiting until the last minute.

Lesson 40: Responding to Failure

1. Did I fail?

2. Why did I fail?

3. What can I do to prevent failing next time?

4. What do I do now?

   a. Try again.

   b. Do something else.

   c. Ask for help.

RELIEVING STRESS

Lesson 41: Handling Accusations

Objective: Students will remain calm and respond to accusations.

Materials Needed: None.

Establish the Need: Ask for volunteers to perform a skit. Arrange with one student ahead of time that you will unjustly accuse him of stealing the stopwatch off your desk. Later you find the stopwatch in your drawer. (1) What was unfair? (2) Have you ever been accused of something? (3) Discuss.

Procedures:

Step 1: Model the skill:

Model using "Think Aloud" strategies—the accusation by a coworker that you did not put a projector back.

1. What am I accused of?
2. Why am I being accused?
3. How do I respond?
   a. Deny it.
   b. Explain my behavior.
   c. Assert myself.
   d. Apologize.
   e. Offer to correct my wrongdoing.
4. Choose the best one and do it.

Helpful Hints: Accusations from an authority figure are often harder to handle. Discuss.

Step 2: Role play with feedback:

A. In groups, have your students role play being accused using "Think Aloud" strategies.

B. You are accused of lying. Respond. Rotate and discuss.

Helpful Hints: Possible scenarios: Your brother accuses you of wearing his clothes, your parents accuse you of lying, your teacher accuses you of hitting someone.

Step 3: Transfer training:

A. **School:** Ask other teachers or staff to accuse your students and reinforce correct responses.

B. **Home/Community:** Your mother accuses you of breaking a lamp. Discuss.

C. **Peers:** Your friend accuses you of starting a rumor about him or her. Discuss.

Comments: It is important for students to see the importance of admitting to and making retribution for violations.

Extended Activities: (1) Create a mock trial in which someone is accused of something. (2) This lesson could tie in with a lesson on our court system, freedom of speech, and so forth. (3) Your students could research examples in history when wrongly accused people had no recourse. "Handling Stress Award," page 94 and "Homework Form," page 14.

Lesson 41: Handling Accusations

1. What am I accused of?

2. Why am I being accused?

3. How do I respond?
   a. Deny it.
   b. Explain my behavior.
   c. Assert myself.
   d. Apologize.
   e. Offer to correct my wrongdoing.

4. Choose the best one and do it.

RELIEVING STRESS

Lesson 42: Finding Something to Do

Objective: Students will choose an activity to do when done with their work.

Materials Needed: Activities to do when done with work.

Establish the Need: Read this story: *"Zach was done with his math sheet before most of the class. He was bored and couldn't think of anything to do, so he wadded pieces of paper and threw them at David. Ms. Winkler saw him and became angry. She yelled at him and made him pick up the papers."* (1) Did Zach make a good choice in finding something to do? (2) What other choices might he have made?

Procedures:

Step 1: Model the skill:

Model using "Think Aloud" strategies—finding something to do when you are done with your work.

1. Am I done?
2. Do I need to recheck my work?
3. What can I do now?

Helpful Hints: Brainstorm appropriate activities to do when finished with your work.

Step 2: Role play with feedback:

A. Assign short worksheets after discussing with your students appropriate activities to do when done.

B. Role play finding something to do when you complete your work. Some people read or find other unfinished work.

Helpful Hints: Reinforce your students for making good choices. What would happen if students completed their work and then disrupted the class?

Step 3: Transfer training:

A. **School:** Ask fellow teachers to reinforce students for choosing an appropriate activity when done with their work.

B. **Home/Community:** All your friends are busy and there is nothing good on TV. What can you do?

C. **Peers:** Your friend has to stay in at recess. What do you do?

Comments: Learning Centers are a wonderful activity for you to provide your students to use after completing other work.

Extended Activities: (1) Make a list of all the things you can do in your class when you are done with your work. (2) Make a list of those things you can do at home. (3) In small groups, share ideas from the list. "Decision Making Award," page 118 and "Homework Form," page 14.

Lesson 42: Finding Something to Do

1. Am I done?

2. Do I need to recheck my work?

3. What can I do now?

MAKING DECISIONS

Decision Making Award

to

_____

for using the skill of

_____

Date _____

Signed _____

Lesson 43: Is It My Problem?

Objective: Students will identify the problem and determine ownership.

Materials Needed: Ideas for scenarios.

Establish the Need: Read this story: *"Beth was upset. She had just learned last night that her family was moving to Toronto. Mary invites Beth to play soccer at recess. Beth snaps at Mary and stomps away in tears."* (1) What is the problem? (2) What might Mary do?

Procedures:

Step 1: Model the skill:

Model using "Think Aloud" strategies—Is it your problem that the secretary yelled at you or you were late to school?

1. What is the problem?
2. Did I cause it?
3. Can I solve it?
4. Do I want to?

Helpful Hints: It would be good to model an example of a problem you are responsible for and one you are not.

Step 2: Role play with feedback:

A. Role play in groups using "Think Aloud" strategies.

B. Role play a problem—copying someone's answers to homework. Discuss the results.

Helpful Hints: Brainstorm possible problems to be role played. Student might role play—causing a problem, (i.e., stealing) and then trying to deny it. Discuss.

Step 3: Transfer training:

A. **School:** All the equipment is gone in P.E. and you are left without any.

B. **Home/Community:** Your mom burns the toast and yells at you. Is it your problem? Discuss.

C. **Peers:** Steve is angry that he didn't get invited to a neighborhood party. Is it your problem?

Comments: The purpose of this lesson is to help your students decide which problems they are responsible for and which they aren't. They need to see that some problems are beyond their control, but to accept responsibility for problems they create.

Extended Activities: (1) Compile a list of scenarios. Have your students determine whose problem each is and what might be done. (2) Discuss current events, local or national, describing a problem and have them determine whose problem it is and what could be done. "Decision Making Award," page 118 and "Homework Form," page 14.

Lesson 43: Is It My Problem?

1. What is the problem?

2. Did I cause it?

3. Can I solve it?

4. Do I want to?

MAKING DECISIONS

Lesson 44: Goal Setting

Objective: Students will set and attain realistic goals.

Materials Needed: None.

Establish the Need: Read this story: *"Dennis never gave any thought to what he might want to do with his life. He spent a lot of time playing, spent all the money he earned, and didn't work hard to do well in school. David wanted to be a surgeon when he grew up. He knew college would be expensive, so he had a paper route and saved his money. He knew he would have to have good grades to be accepted, so he worked hard in school and did well."*

Procedures:

Step 1: Model the skill:

Model using "Think Aloud" strategies—making a goal.

1. What goal do I want to reach?
2. Find out all I can about my goal.
3. What steps must I take to reach my goal?
4. Do it.

Helpful Hints: Explain there are long-term and short-term goals and importance of each.

Step 2: Role play with feedback:

A. Brainstorm ideas for short-term goals. Then have each student write a goal and the steps needed to reach it.

B. Goal is to improve grade in math. What is my next step?

Helpful Hints: This might be a good activity for cooperative learning groups. You want to exercise daily, but find you are too busy. Was your goal realistic? Do we set goals for ourselves that can't be reached?

Step 3: Transfer training:

A. **School:** Have each student set one short-term goal for school.

B. **Home/Community:** Each student will set one short-term goal for home.

C. **Peers:** Each student will set one short-term goal with a friend.

Comments: Discuss with your students the need to reward themselves and/or celebrate completing a goal. Completing goals is a way to enhance self-esteem and can be particularly beneficial for those children who lack self-esteem.

Extended Activities: (1) Discuss and establish a goal for the whole class. Plan the reward for reaching the goal. (2) Have your students write up one long-term goal they would like to reach and the steps needed to accomplish it. What about dreaming that you are rich and famous? Can dreams turn into goals? "Decision Making Award," page 118 and "Homework Form," page 14.

Making Decisions

Lesson 44: Goal Setting

1. What goal do I want to reach?

2. Find out all I can about my goal.

3. What steps must I take to reach my goal?

4. Do it.

MAKING DECISIONS

Lesson 45: What are My Abilities?

Objective: Students will list at least one quality which is a strength.

Materials Needed: Individual goals from the previous lesson.

Establish the Need: Read this story: *"Sheila wanted to set a goal of trying out for a community play. She had never been in a play before and wondered if she could do it. She decided to ask her fourth grade teacher if he thought she had the ability to do the part."*

Procedures:

Step 1: Model the skill:

Model using "Think Aloud" strategies—deciding if you have the ability to take ballet lessons.

1. What ability is needed?
2. How did I do with a similar task?
3. Ask other people about my ability.
4. Do I want to do it?

Helpful Hints: Some students will have unrealistic ideas about their abilities. Some need to be reaffirmed that they have the ability to do a task.

Step 2: Role play with feedback:

A. In small groups, have your students discuss goals from the previous lesson and give feedback to each other on their ability to reach the goal.

B. Discuss one ability that is your strength.

Helpful Hints: What weakness do you have that hinders your strengths?

Step 3: Transfer training:

A. **School:** I want to make the most points in soccer. Do I have the ability?

B. **Home/Community:** I want to cook dinner. Do I have the ability?

C. **Peers:** I want to invite a friend to stay overnight. Do I have the ability?

Comments: The intention of this lesson is to assist students to evaluate their capabilities realistically so they have a better chance at achieving the goals they set.

Extended Activities: (1) Have your students list things they could do to improve their ability to reach a goal they want. (2) Journal about student's abilities and how they want to use them. "Decision Making Award," page 118 and "Homework Form," page 14.

Making Decisions

Lesson 45: What are My Abilities?

1. What ability is needed?

2. How did I do with a similar task?

3. Ask other people about my ability.

4. Do I want to do it?

MAKING DECISIONS

       Dennis Hanken, Ed.S. and Judith Kennedy, Ed.S.

Lesson 46: Gathering Information

Objective: Students will list sources of information.

Materials Needed: Access to library.

Establish the Need: Read this story: *"Alex wanted to buy a new compact disc, but the store he usually went to didn't have the one he wanted."* (1) List the sources he could seek for finding the CD.

Procedures:

Step 1: Model the skill:

Model using "Think Aloud" strategies—finding information about something you are interested in.

1. What information do I need?
2. Where can I find the information?
   a. People.
   b. Books, telephone calls.
   c. Library/internet.
3. Find it.

Helpful Hints: Your students may need help in listing all the many sources for finding information.

Step 2: Role play with feedback:

A. Assign the task of finding information on something using the library. Students may work in pairs.

B. Role play finding information in certain books. Are these books an authority in that field?

Helpful Hints: You may use a timely topic such as history of a holiday, or sport, or origin of a custom. Should we believe everything we read in a newspaper?

Step 3: Transfer training:

A. **School:** How do you find out what the nurse at school does?

B. **Home/Community:** How do you find what churches are in your neighborhood?

C. **Peers:** How to locate the house of your friend?

Comments: Successfully accessing information is a vital life skill.

Extended Activities: (1) Where in town would you find ski wear? (2) Where can you rent a bike? (3) Where might you find where to play tennis? "Decision Making Award," page 118 and "Homework Form," page 14.

Making Decisions

Lesson 46: Gathering Information

1. What information do I need?

2. Where can I find the information?

a. People.

b. Books, telephone calls.

c. Library/internet.

3. Find it.

MAKING DECISIONS

Lesson 47: Prioritizing Activities

Objective: Students will list and prioritize personal activities and obligations.

Materials Needed: None.

Establish the Need: Read this story: *"Stewart stewed and stewed about getting his homework done, doing his chores, watching a TV program he liked or riding bikes with a friend. He couldn't decide what to do first."*

Procedures:

Step 1: Model the skill:

Model using "Think Aloud" strategies—prioritizing some activities related to class schedules.

1. Think about the options.
2. List the activities from most to least importance.
3. Decide the order for doing them.

Helpful Hints: This skill is to help students who can't decide what to start on first.

Step 2: Role play with feedback:

A. Have your students think about their activities, list from most to least important, plan steps to deal with them.

B. Role play planning your homework when you have homework and a test in four of your classes.

Helpful Hints: You may need to discuss this as a class or work in groups. What happens when you are disorganized and flighty?

Step 3: Transfer training:

A. **School:** You have homework in every class. What do you do first?

B. **Home/Community:** You have to do the dishes and carry out trash. What do you do first?

C. **Peers:** You are invited to go somewhere with two different friends. What do you do?

Comments: You may need to help your students see that they sometimes need to do what they don't like first, then schedule fun things.

Extended Activities: (1) In a class meeting, discuss and prioritize a schedule and plan steps for dealing with it. (2) Prioritize problems in the school district or community and elicit steps that could be taken to solve them. "Decision Making Award," page 118 and "Homework Form," page 14.

Lesson 47: Prioritizing Activities

1. Think about the options.

2. List the activities from most to least importance.

3. Decide the order for doing them.

MAKING DECISIONS

Lesson 48: Making the Best Decision

Objective: Students will perform the decision-making model.

Materials Needed: None.

Establish the Need: Read this story: *"Rebecca was asked to go to the game with Susan, the mall with Elizabeth, and the movie with Diane. She wanted to do each one and she didn't want to disappoint any of her friends."* (1) How will Rebecca make her decision? (2) What are some consequences she may face in making this decision?

Procedures:

Step 1: Model the skill:

Model using "Think Aloud" strategies—making a decision.

1. What is the situation?
2. Name three decisions I could make.
3. Name the consequences or rewards of each.
4. Act on the best choice.

Helpful Hints: It is important for your students to name three decisions to get them out of the either/or mind frame.

Step 2: Role play with feedback:

A. Introduce this scenario: You have been invited to ride bikes with friends after school, but you have math homework to do for tomorrow and your favorite TV shows are on tonight. Make a decision using "Think Aloud" strategies.

B. Role play making a good decision and a bad decision in choosing a friend. Discuss.

Helpful Hints: Help your students see that sometimes our choices are among ones we would not prefer, but we need to decide based on consequences and preferences. What happens when you make poor decisions? Give examples from your own life. Discuss.

Step 3: Transfer training:

A. **School:** You want to go to computer science, but need to finish a social studies worksheet.

B. **Home/Community:** You want to join your friends outside before it gets dark, but it's your turn to do the dishes.

C. **Peers:** You want to invite a friend over, but haven't cleaned your room.

Helpful Hints: It would be helpful to lead your students in a discussion to see the advantages of work first, then play.

Comments: This is an important life skill and teaches responsibility and consequences.

Extended Activities: (1) Design a skit showing the decision-making model. (2) Brainstorm a scenario and, as a class, list choices and consequences. (3) Use the decision-making model for individual and class decisions on an everyday basis. (3) Students come up with decision scenarios to be used in the next lesson. "Decision Making Award," page 118 and "Homework Form," page 14.

Making Decisions

Lesson 48: Making a Decision

1. What is the situation?

2. Name three decisions I could make.

3. Name the consequences or rewards of each.

4. Act on the best choice.

MAKING DECISIONS

Lesson 49: Concentrating on a Task

Objective: Students will remain on a task until it is completed.

Materials Needed: Students' decision plans from previous lesson.

Establish the Need: Read this story: *"Jeff needed to decide whether to save his money, use it to go to a movie with Brad, or buy his mother a birthday gift. He used the decision-making model and decided buying his mother the birthday gift had the fewest consequences, but he never did get around to going to the store to buy it."*

    1. The choice seemed right, but what about the follow through?

    2. Did Jeff make the right choice?

Procedures:

Step 1: Model the skill:

Model using "Think Aloud" strategies—concentrating on a task to complete a decision you made.

    1. What was my decision?

    2. What steps do I need to take to do it?

        a. Ignore distractions.

        b. Follow the task to completion.

    3. Do it.

Helpful Hints: Your students may need examples to see that the best decisions in the world are no good if they are not followed by action.

Step 2: Role play with feedback:

A. Using previous decision-making scenarios, have them state using "Think Aloud" strategies how to concentrate on a task until done.

B. Role play what concentration is involved in doing a task.

Helpful Hints: For students who lack perseverance, it will be important that action steps are manageable. When you lose concentration on a task and don't complete it, discuss results.

Step 3: Transfer training:

A. **School:** What steps do you need to take to concentrate and complete your science project?

B. **Home/Community:** What steps do you need to take to clean your room?

C. **Peers:** What steps do you need to take to make a new friend?

Comments: This differs from distractibility in the class in that it is concentrating on a goal until it is achieved.

Extended Activities: (1) What steps would you need to take to attend college? (2) How will you concentrate and complete this school year? "Decision Making Award," page 118 and "Homework Form," page 14.

Lesson 49: Concentrating on a Task

1. What was my decision?

2. What steps do I need to take to do it?

a. Ignore distractions.

b. Follow the task to completion.

3. Do it.

MAKING DECISIONS

Lesson 50: Expressing Anger in Appropriate Ways

Objective: Students will be able to express anger in appropriate ways.

Materials Needed: None.

Establish the Need: Read the stories, "The Horse and the Laden Donkey" and "Anger and Other Choices," on the next page.

Procedures:

Step 1: Model the skill:

A. Set up a scenario where you are angry.

B. Use "Think Aloud" strategies to model appropriate ways to express anger.

    1. Stop and count to five.

    2. Think about why I am angry.

    3. Choose.

        a. Tell the person why I am angry.

        b. Walk away.

        c. Take five deep breaths.

        d. Write or draw how I feel.

    4. Make the right choice.

Helpful Hints: Anger is a powerful emotion which everyone needs to handle. It is important to teach students that feeling angry is normal, but we need to be responsible for how we act when angry.

Step 2: Role play with feedback:

A. Role play in groups of three different scenarios (see helpful hints). How would you express anger in each situation? Don't forget to use "Think Aloud" strategies. Rotate and give feedback.

B. Role play in groups of three using personal experiences. (Explain what happened when you got angry.) Discuss positive results.

Helpful Hints: Suggested scenarios: (1) Your best friend left town. (2) Your parents punished you when your brother or sister actually did it. (3) You forgot your homework. (4) You lost an expensive birthday gift. (5) You got hit with a snowball. Students role play what happens when they lose their temper and say and do things they may regret.

Step 3: Transfer training:

A. **School:** You were put in the first seat by the teacher because you can't be trusted.

B. **Home/Community:** You broke the window next door and had to spend all your allowance for it.

C. **Peers:** Your best friend won't talk to you anymore.

Comments: Discuss what anger is and how all of us deal with it differently.

Extended Activities: Make a list of the signs of getting angry, i.e., getting tense, jaw clenching, fidgety, illogical thoughts, name calling, withdrawing. Also talk about what behavior is rational or natural. Discuss cause and effect. Discuss consequences for our actions and taking responsibility. "Homework Form," page 14 and "Self-Control Award," page 136.

The Horse and the Laden Donkey

Once there was a man who kept a horse and a donkey as beasts of burden. It was his custom to load the donkey until he could barely stagger under the weight, while the horse was allowed to prance along in its fine trappings with a very light load.

As they were preceding along the road one day, the donkey, who had been ailing for the past several days, said to the horse, "Will you relieve me of part of my load for a few miles? I feel dreadfully unwell, but if you will carry a fair portion of the freight today, I shall soon get well again. This weight is killing me." The horse, however, merely kicked up his heels and told the donkey not to trouble him with his complaints. The donkey staggered along for another half mile in silence, then suddenly fell to the ground dead. Just then the master came up and perceiving what happened, he removed the load from the dead donkey and placed it on the horses back, "Alas," groaned the horse, as he started off with the heavy load augmented by the carcass of the dead donkey, now am I rewarded for my ill-nature by refusing to bear my fair share of the load. I now must carry the whole of it plus the dead weight of my poor companion.

Application: A bad temper carries with it its own punishment.

Anger and Other Choices

Dennis wanted to play soccer at recess. When it was recess time, he leapt out of his desk to grab his soccer ball and head for the field. His teacher, Mrs. Fields, stopped him and said, "Dennis, you cannot go to recess until you finish your math worksheet." Dennis sat down angrily and finished his math as fast as he could. He tossed it on Mrs. Fields' desk and streaked outside with his ball. He found the soccer teams were already formed, and they wouldn't let him join. He was so angry he threw his soccer ball at the goalie. The playground supervisor saw him do it and sent him in to his class.

1. What were some other choices he could have made?
2. What suggestions do you have for Dennis for controlling his anger?

Lesson 50: Expressing Anger in Appropriate Ways

1. Stop and count to five.

2. Think about why I am angry.

3. Choose:
   a. Tell the person why I am angry.
   b. Walk away.
   c. Take five deep breaths.

4. Write or draw how I feel.

5. Make the right choice.

REPLACEMENT SKILLS

Self-Control
Award
to

_____

for using the skill of

_____

Date _____

*Signature*_____

Lesson 51: Avoiding Fights

Objective: Students will be able to recognize a conflict and try to avoid a physical and verbal fight.

Materials Needed: None.

Establish the Need: *"John and Ben both wanted to play with the only remaining soccer ball. John grabbed it and ran. Ben chased him, knocked him down, hit him and got the ball. Both boys were sent to the principal by the playground supervisor."* (1) What was the problem? (2) What other ways could they have solved it? (3) What is the best choice? (4) What are some ways to avoid fights?

Procedures:

Step 1: Model the skill:

Using "Think Aloud" strategies, model the skill—

1. Stop and think. Do I want to fight?
2. Choose:
   a. Walk away.
   b. Talk to the person and resolve the problem.
   c. Ask someone to help solve the problem.
   d. Yell for help and run away.
   e. Stand up to the person.

Helpful Hints: Discuss the consequences of fighting, hurting someone, and getting into trouble. Talk about different ways to handle conflict.

Step 2: Role play with feedback:

A. Using a given scenario (see Helpful Hints), role play using "Think Aloud" strategies avoiding fights (in groups of three). Rotate roles.

B. Discuss why fighting is a poor solution to a problem.

Helpful Hints: Discuss a conflict on the playground that resulted in a fight. Different scenarios: pushed in line, called names, not sharing, protecting a friend.

Step 3: Transfer training:

A. **School:** Someone pushes you on the playground. You call that person a name. What happens next?

B. **Home/Community:** Someone takes your bike for a joyride. What should you do?

C. **Peers:** A bully in your class picks a fight with your best friend. Should you help?

Comments: Discuss boxing, karate, and the need to defend yourself. Is this different from avoiding fights? How does TV violence impact this skill?

Extended Activities: Make up a series of plays depicting conflict situations where characters use "Think Aloud" strategies to avoid fights. "Homework Form," page 14 and "Self-Control Award," page 136.

Replacement Skills

Lesson 51: Avoiding Fights

1. Stop and think.
   Do I want to fight?

2. Choose:

   a. Walk away.

   b. Talk to the person and resolve the problem.

   c. Ask someone to help solve the problem.

   d. Yell for help and run away.

   e. Stand up to the person.

REPLACEMENT SKILLS

Lesson 52: Asking Permission

Objective:	Students will be able to ask permission appropriately.
Materials Needed:	None.
Establish the Need:	Read the story on the next page, "Betty and the Birthday Party."
Procedures:	

Step 1: Model the skill:

Using "Think Aloud" strategies, model the skill.

1. What do I need permission for?
2. Who do I have to ask?
3. Decide how to—
   a. Ask out loud in a group.
   b. Ask privately.
   c. Ask in writing.
4. Choose the right time and place.
5. Ask.

Helpful Hints: Tone of voice is very important.

Step 2: Role play with feedback:

A. Role play in groups of two, asking permission. Rotate and give feedback. (Brainstorm in large group what to ask for.)

B. Role play asking permission from peers. Rotate and give feedback.

Helpful Hints: Count how many times you have to ask for permission in a day, i.e., teachers, parent, adults, and so forth. Ask permission in a negative way and compare results. What happens when you do something without permission?

Step 3: Transfer training:

A. **School:** Ask permission to go to the library, bathroom, or use the phone.

B. **Home/Community:** Ask permission from parents to stay overnight at a friend's house.

C. **Peers:** Ask permission to borrow some money for lunch.

Comments: Don't expect favors from others if you never give any. Some people have trouble asking for permission. Discuss refusals and how to handle them.

Extended Activities: If you are sincere about asking, people will more likely understand. How do you feel when you are turned down when you ask? How should you react? Discuss. Journal how you feel when you ask for permission and are refused. Why were you refused? What could you do to avoid refusal in the future? "Homework Form," page 14 and "Self-Control Award," page 136.

Replacement Skills

Betty and the Birthday Party

Betty was a fifth grade student who wanted to have both boys and girls at her birthday party, but only have the girls stay over night. She knew that her mom and dad would not allow this. She figured if I ask nice and keep an open mind maybe my parents will say "yes." She asked, but her parents would only agree to ten friends, but no boys. Betty was really mad, but she waited a couple of days to ask again. Her parents and she decided to compromise, she could invite five boys and five girls to a pizza party. Asking permission may not always get the desired results, but if you keep talking and compromise, you may come to a good resolution.

Lesson 52: Asking Permission

1. What do I need permission for?

2. Who do I have to ask?

3. Decide how to—

   a. Ask out loud in a group.

   b. Ask privately.

   c. Ask in writing.

4. Choose the right time and place.

5. Ask.

REPLACEMENT SKILLS

Lesson 53: Sharing

Objective: Student will be able to share items with peers or adults.

Materials Needed: None.

Establish the Need: Read the fable, "The Travelers and the Hatchet," on the next page.

Procedures:

Step 1: Model the skill:

Using "Think Aloud" strategies, model the skill.

1. Decide if I want to share.
2. Think about how that person will react to my sharing.
   a. Agree.
   b. Insulted.
   c. Pleased.
   d. Suspicious.
3. Offer to share in a friendly and appropriate way.
4. The response may be a decline or an acceptance—make an appropriate comment.

Helpful Hints: Help your students determine when it is appropriate to share. Does someone need something I can give them without causing myself a problem?

Step 2: Role play with feedback:

A. Role play sharing items in groups of two. Rotate and give feedback.

B. Role play accepting something somebody wants to share with you. Rotate and give feedback.

Helpful Hints: Role play not sharing. What does the word "stingy" or "selfish" mean to you?

Step 3: Transfer training:

A. **School:** Share your note paper with a student who forgot to bring paper.

B. **Home/Community:** Share your Nintendo with a friend.

C. **Peers:** Share some candy with your friends.

Comments: Is it difficult to share things with family members, but okay to share with friends?

Extended Activities: Sometimes we don't like to share. Talk about the satisfaction of sharing and helping someone. Have your students draw a picture of a situation where they chose to share and how they felt. "Homework Form," page 14 and "Self-Control Award," page 136.

Replacement Skills

The Travelers and the Hatchet

Two men were traveling along the highroad toward the town. Suddenly one of them spied a hatchet half hidden in the fallen leaves. "Look what I have found!," he cried, picking up the tool. "Do not say 'I,'" replied his companion. It is more proper to say, "Look what we have found!" The finder of the hatchet shrugged his shoulders and they continued on their way. Presently they came upon a group of men whose eyes were on the roadway as though they were looking for something. Suddenly one of the strangers pointed to the approaching twain, and they rushed up to them, pointing to the hatchet. "Alas," said the traveler who had found the hatchet, "It looks as though we are in trouble." What do you mean 'we are in trouble'? What you really mean to say is that 'I am in trouble!'"

Application: He who will not allow his friend to share the prize must not expect him to share the danger.

1. Do you know people who only want to share the good times?
2. Is it easy or hard for you to share?

Lesson 53: Sharing

1. Decide if I want to share.

2. Think about how that person will react to my sharing.
   a. Agree.
   b. Insulted.
   c. Pleased.
   d. Suspicious.

3. Offer to share in a friendly and appropriate way.

4. The response may be a decline or an acceptance—make an appropriate comment.

REPLACEMENT SKILLS

Dennis Hanken, Ed.S. and Judith Kennedy, Ed.S.

Lesson 54: Helping Others

Objective: Students will be able to help others in a friendly way.

Materials Needed: None.

Establish the Need: Read the stories, "The Eagle and the Fox" and "Helping a Friend," on the next page.

Procedures:

Step 1: Model the skill:

Using "Think Aloud" strategies—

1. Decide if the other person needs and wants your help.
2. Think of ways you could be helpful.
3. Ask the other person if he or she needs and wants your help.
4. Help the other person.

Helpful Hints: For overly helpful students, you may need to reinforce the need to ask if the other person wants help.

Step 2: Role play with feedback:

A. Role play helping friends or family carry groceries into the house. Rotate and give feedback.

B. Role play helping the teacher during different times of the day. Discuss and give feedback. Are you the teacher's "pet" if you help the teacher?

C. Role play helping someone who is feeling sad.

Helpful Hints: Scenarios for helping others. (1) When someone is sick. (2) When someone is feeling bad. (3) When someone needs a friend. (4) When someone is being teased. Discuss when you *don't* help people.

Step 3: Transfer training:

A. **School:** Help a student clean the blackboard.

B. **Home/Community:** Help a neighbor rake leaves or sweep the sidewalk.

C. **Peers:** Help a friend with his or her homework.

Comments: When people help others in the community, it makes the community a better place. Explain.

Extended Activities: Helping others who are less fortunate than you is an act of kindness. Being kind is not showing you are weak, it is being considerate of others. Would you like to be treated the same way? Arrange for the class to do a helpful activity for the community. Brainstorm ideas (visit home for elderly, pick someone in need and mow their lawn, etc.). Let your class choose the activity. Discuss afterward. "Homework Form," page 14 and "Self-Control Award," page 136.

The Eagle and the Fox

An eagle and a fox long had lived together as good neighbors, the eagle at the top of a high tree and the fox in a hole at the foot of it. One day, however, while the fox was away, the eagle, seeking a tender morsel for her nestful of young ones, swooped down upon the fox's cub and carried it way to her nest. The fox, on her return home, upbraided the eagle for his breach of friendship, and pleaded with the eagle to return the cub to her den. But the eagle, feeling sure that her own brood high up in the treetop nest were safe from any possible revenge, ignored the entreaties of the cub's mother.

Quickly running to the place where she knew an altar fire to be burning, the fox snatched a branch and hurried back to the tree. The mother eagle, who was just on the point of tearing the cub to pieces to feed her babies, looked down and saw that the fox was going to set fire to the tree and burn it and her nest and the baby eagles to ashes. "Hold on, dear neighbor!" she screamed. Don't set fire to our tree. I'll bring your cub to you safe and sound."

Application: Do unto others as you would have them do unto you.

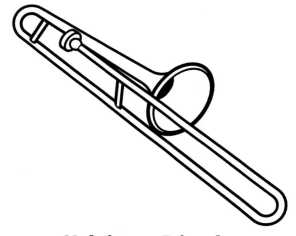

Helping a Friend

Bethany had to carry her trombone home tonight as well as her science and math books. She was struggling to pick it all up and get it balanced for the walk home. She finally picked it all up and started toward the classroom door, but her books slid off her trombone case and clattered to the floor. Emily had been watching this. She asked herself, "Am I willing to help Bethany?" and decided, "yes." She walked up to Bethany and said, "Would you like me to help carry your books?"

Dennis Hanken, Ed.S. and Judith Kennedy, Ed.S.

Lesson 54: Helping Others

1. Decide if the other person needs and wants my help.

2. Think of ways I could be helpful.

3. Ask the other person if he or she wants my help.

4. Help the other person.

REPLACEMENT SKILLS

Lesson 55: Negotiating/Compromising

Objective: Students will recognize differences of opinion and negotiate without getting tense and arguing.

Materials Needed: None.

Establish the Need: Picture yourself as a U.S. Senator and you want to make a law, but you need to have other senators support you. What do you have to do?

Procedures:

Step 1: Model the skill:

Using "Think Aloud" strategies, model the skill:

1. Am I and the other person disagreeing?
2. Tell the other person my opinion of the problem.
3. Ask the other person's opinion.
4. Listen respectfully.
5. Think about the feelings of the other person.
6. Can I compromise?

Helpful Hints: Define "compromise" and "negotiate."

Step 2: Role play with feedback:

A. Role play in small groups negotiating differences of opinions (see helpful hints). Rotate and give feedback.

B. Role play with boys on one side, girls on the other. Does this make a difference in opinions?

Helpful Hints: Philosophically: (1) Religious difference. (2) Political difference. (3) Dropping out of school versus staying in school. What happens to arguments when you can't compromise?

Step 3: Transfer training:

A. **School:** You disagree with a teacher on how to treat others. Negotiate.

B. **Home/Community:** You are fighting over turns on a bike. Negotiate.

C. **Peers:** You are arguing over the best team in the city. Who's the best? Negotiate.

Comments: People don't always value differences in opinions. If you respect others, you need to listen to what they say. It is okay to have different opinions and beliefs.

Extended Activities: This is a life long skill. Why do we need this skill in adulthood? What professionals use this the most? Develop a skit showing a bill introduced into Congress, and the process of negotiation in getting it passed. "Homework Form," page 14 and "Self-Control Award," page 136.

Replacement Skills

Lesson 55: Negotiating

1. Am I and the other person disagreeing?

2. Tell the other person my opinion of the problem.

3. Ask the other person's opinion.

4. Listen respectfully.

5. Think about the feelings of the other person.

6. Can I compromise?

REPLACEMENT SKILLS

Lesson 56: Using Self-Control

Objective: Student will be able to use self-control by recognizing the signs of losing control and changing their behavior.

Materials Needed: None.

Establish the Need: Discuss when a person loses self-control and hurts others. What are the consequences?

Procedures:

Step 1: Model the skill:

Using "Think Aloud" strategies, model the skill:

1. Stop what I am doing.
2. Recognize the changes in my body—tense, body temperature, squirming, nervous, and so forth.
3. What made me feel this way?
4. Think about ways to control myself:
   a. Count to five.
   b. Take three deep breaths.
   c. Do something else.
5. Make a choice and do it.

Helpful Hints: This is a very difficult skill for impulsive people. They will need to make considerable effort to slow down and recognize the symptoms of losing of control.

Step 2: Role play with feedback:

A. Have your students in pairs role play using self-control when they are angry with an adult. Students will watch and give feedback.

B. Have your students demonstrate being in control after being upset. Rotate and give feedback.

Helpful Hints: You may want to give negative examples from TV shows or movies—*Roseanne; Coach*, fights during a baseball or basketball game.

Step 3: Transfer training:

A. **School:** You forgot all your books at home and you can't reach your parents. Use self-control.

B. **Home/Community:** Your parents won't let you go to the mall alone.

C. **Peers:** A friend spreads gossip about you.

Comments: Using self-control can be very beneficial to you as a person. Using self-control gains you respect and you are seen as confident.

Extended Activities: Many people we read about in the newspaper lost control and hurt other people, i.e., shootings in schools or public places, abusing others in families. Might people in jail wish they had used more self-control? Journal about a time you lost control, what were the consequences? What would have been a better choice? "Homework Form," page 14 and "Self-Control Award," page 136.

Lesson 56: Using Self-Control

1. Stop what I am doing.

2. Recognize the changes in my body—tense, body temperature, squirming, nervous, and so forth.

3. What made me feel this way?

4. Think about ways to control myself:
    a. Count to five.
    b. Take three deep breaths.
    c. Do something else.

5. Make a choice and do It.

REPLACEMENT SKILLS

Lesson 57: Standing Up for Your Rights

Objective: Students will be able to recognize and react to their own beliefs and stand up for them.

Materials Needed: None.

Establish the Need: People usually fit into one of two groups: *followers*—they follow the lead of others and rarely stand up for their own rights, and *leaders*—stand up for their rights, are self-confident, and think for themselves. What do you want to be? Give examples of each from famous people.

Procedures:

Step 1: Model the skill:

Using "Think Aloud" strategies, model the skill:

1. Stop and think—do I want to stand up for my rights?
2. Why am I dissatisfied?
3. Think about ways to express my dissatisfaction:
   a. Ask others' help.
   b. Say what is on my mind.
   c. Choose the right time and place.
4. Be direct in a nice manner.

Helpful Hints: Brainstorm scenarios where someone might choose to stand up for his or her rights. What are possible consequences of standing up or not?

Step 2: Role play with feedback:

A. Role play in groups "standing up for something you believe in." Recall sometime in the last six months where you did this. Rotate and discuss.

B. Role play "standing up for your rights" as a student in the classroom. What are your rights and who is going to challenge these rights? Discuss and rotate.

Helpful Hints: Have you ever been in a situation where you have backed down and didn't stand up for your rights? Discuss how our rights sometimes will infringe on others' rights.

Step 3: Transfer training:

A. **School:** You are on a swing for one minute and a bigger person comes over and says, "Get off."

B. **Home/Community:** You are watching TV and your older brother/sister comes and changes the channel.

C. **Peers:** One of your friends accuses you of cheating on a test. You did not cheat.

Comments: Every person has certain rights. Sometimes people will not always come to your rescue, so you will have to stand up for your own rights.

Extended Activities: (1) Have your students write letters, real or fictional, to a business where they got a defective product. (2) Brainstorm an appropriate cause in the school or town, and students write in support of chosen one. "Homework Form," page 14 and "Self-Control Award," page 136.

Replacement Skills

Lesson 57: Standing Up for Your Rights

1. Stop and think—do I want to stand up for my rights?

2. Why am I dissatisfied?

3. Think about ways to express my dissatisfaction:

    a. Ask others' help.
    b. Say what is on my mind.
    c. Choose the right time and place.

4. Be direct in a nice manner.

REPLACEMENT SKILLS

Lesson 58: Avoiding Trouble with Others

Objective: Students will be able to recognize a bad situation and make a good choice to avoid trouble.

Materials Needed: None.

Establish the Need: Read the stories, "The Lion and His Three Counselors" and "Almost a Problem," on the next page.

Procedures:

Step 1: Model the skill:

Using "Think Aloud" strategies, model the skill:

1. Decide if I want to avoid trouble.
2. Inform others what I want to do.
3. Suggest other alternatives.
4. Make a good choice.

Helpful Hints: Give some personal examples where you have had to make choices to avoid trouble.

Step 2: Role play with feedback:

A. Role play in groups different scenarios where you can avoid trouble. Rotate and discuss.

B. Role play using different situations (see below) and use "Think Aloud" strategies. Discuss the results.

Helpful Hints: Role play a situation (joining a gang) where you try to avoid a problem. (1) Stealing something. (2) Cheating on a test. (3) Lying. (4) Gossip.

Step 3: Transfer training:

A. **School:** You are asked to pick on a student who wears funny clothes.

B. **Home/Community:** A group of kids ask you to help them beat-up someone.

C. **Peers:** Your best friend asks you to join him or her in a cigarette.

Comments: If you think about long-range consequences, this helps you avoid trouble.

Extended Activities: You need to weigh the risks versus the gains. This is a good time to talk about good choices and bad choices. (1) List troublesome situations by brainstorming. Have your students write alternative choices for each. (2) Create a skit with this theme to portray for a younger class. "Homework Form," page 14 and "Self-Control Award," page 136.

The Lion and His Three Counselors

The King of Beasts was in an irritable mood. That morning his mate had told him that his breath was most unpleasant. After doing considerable roaring to prove that he was king, he summoned his counselors.

First he called the sheep. "Friend sheep," he roared, opening wide his great mouth, "would you say that my breath smells unpleasant?"

Believing that the lion wanted his honest answer, the sheep gave it, and the king of beasts bit off his head for being a fool.

Then he called the wolf and asked him the same question. The wolf catching sight of the carcass of the sheep, said, "Why, your majesty, you have a breath as sweet as blossoms in the spring...." Before he could finish he had been torn to pieces for a flatterer.

At last the lion called the fox and put the question to him. The fox gave a hollow cough, then cleared his throat, "Your majesty," he whispered, "truly, I have such a cold in the head that I cannot smell at all."

Application: In dangerous times, wise men say nothing.

1. When someone is mad, should that person be left alone? Discuss.

2. When you are angry, do you still need to be in control?

Almost a Problem

John, a fifth grader, was getting a drink of water in the hallway on a warm September afternoon. Greg, the bully of the sixth grade class, came by John and pushed him in the back. John did not appreciate this and told Greg to "stop it." Greg came back to John and stood by him hoping that John would start something. John told him that he was not afraid of him and told him that he did it just to get him in trouble. John then just walked away. Greg stared at him, but let him walk away.

1. Discuss the results and what could have happened?

2. How can you stand up for yourself even when you are afraid?

Replacement Skills

Lesson 58: Avoiding Trouble with Others

1. Decide if I want to avoid trouble.

2. Inform others what I want to do.

3. Suggest other alternatives.

4. Make a good choice.

REPLACEMENT SKILLS

Lesson 59: Responding to Accusations

Objective: Students will be able to respond to accusations in a firm, but direct way and either deny it or apologize and make retribution.

Materials Needed: List of accusations.

Establish the Need: Respond to this accusation. "You are a copy cat, everything I do, you copy." You don't agree and you need to respond. Write down your response. Discuss in class. Save this and go over this skill; then talk about how you handled this. Did you do a good job with the accusation?

Procedures:

Step 1: Model the skill:

Using "Think Aloud" strategies, model the skill:

1. What am I accused of?
2. Why did that person accuse me?
3. How do I answer the accusation? Choices:
   a. Deny it.
   b. Explain my behavior.
   c. Apologize.
   d. Make restitution.
   e. Correct the person's perceptions.

Helpful Hints: Also include the importance of being truthful.

Step 2: Role play with feedback:

A. Role play in groups by having your students think of something they were unjustly accused of and respond. Discuss.

B. Role play in groups by having each person respond to an actual accusation. Discuss.

Helpful Hints: Role play the incorrect way to respond to an accusation. Accuse them of something, be nasty, walk away, argue, lie.

Step 3: Transfer training:

A. **School:** The teacher thinks you cheated on a quiz.

B. **Home/Community:** Your next door neighbor thinks you broke his or her window.

C. **Peers:** Your best friend thinks you stole his or her book.

Comments: Somebody is always blaming somebody for doing things wrong. Discuss how you can avoid accusations, or can you?

Extended Activities: Standing up for your rights will help you with this skill. List accusations and practice responding:

talking during a test	skipping school
destroying school property	smoking on the grounds
lying to the teacher	

"Homework Form," page 14 and "Self-Control Award," page 136.

Lesson 59: Responding to Accusations

1. What am I accused of?

2. Why did that person accuse me?

3. How do I answer the accusation?

Choices:
a. Deny it.
b. Explain my behavior.
c. Apologize.
d. Make restitution.
e. Correct the person's perceptions.

REPLACEMENT SKILLS

Lesson 60: Responding to Intimidation (Bullying)

Objective: Students will be able to recognize intimidation or bullying and respond in an appropriate manner.

Materials Needed: None.

Establish the Need: Read the story, "The Wind and the Sun," on the next page.

Procedures:

Step 1: Model the skill:

Using "Think Aloud" strategies, model the skill:

1. Stop and think—Is this person trying to intimidate me?
2. What are my choices:
    a. Walk away.
    b. Ignore.
    c. Defend myself.
    d. Tell an adult.
3. Try not to show fear.
4. Make the best choice.
5. After the situation, process with an adult.

Helpful Hints: Bullying can become dangerous. Help your students see that behind bullying is fear. Assertiveness is the best way to counteract bullies.

Step 2: Role play with feedback:

A. Role play in groups. What is a bully? What do they try to do to you? Discuss the results.

B. Role play in groups responding to a bully on the playground. (Older, bigger boy.)

Helpful Hints: Can girls be bullies?

Step 3: Transfer training:

A. **School:** An older child on the playground threatens to beat you up after school.

B. **Home/Community:** A neighbor boy tells you your Walkman is his and takes it.

C. **Peers:** One of your friends decides he doesn't like you anymore and tells your other friends not to play with you anymore.

Comments: Bullies probably figure nobody will challenge them, so they will continue to bully until someone stands up to them.

Extended Activities: Discuss being scared or being afraid of someone bigger than you are. (1) Have your students journal about a situation in which they were the bully. (2) Divide in groups and have groups come up with as many ideas as they can for handling bullies. (3) Solicit from your students if they are being bullied and obtain support from other classmates for that person. "Homework Form," page 14 and "Self-Control Award," page 136.

Replacement Skills

The Wind and the Sun

A dispute once arose between the wind and the sun over which was the stronger of the two. There seemed to be no way of settling the issue. But, suddenly they saw a traveler coming down the road.

"This is our chance," said the sun, "to prove who is right. Whichever of us can make that man take off his coat shall be the stronger. And just to show you how sure I am, I'll let you have the first chance." So the sun hid behind the cloud, and the wind blew an icy blast. But the harder he blew the more closely did the traveler wrap his coat around him. At last the wind had to give up in disgust. Then the sun came out from behind the cloud and began to shine down upon the traveler with all his power. The traveler felt the sun's genial warmth, and as he grew warmer and warmer he began to loosen his coat. Finally he was forced to take it off altogether and to sit down in the shade of a tree and fan himself. So the sun was right after all!!

Application: Persuasion is better than Force.

1. Do you try to persuade people by physical force or by talking?
2. Does physical force change their mind because of fear or reason?

Lesson 60: Responding to Intimidation (Bullying)

1. Stop and think—Is this person trying to intimidate me?

2. What are my choices:
   a. Walk away.
   b. Ignore.
   c. Defend myself.
   d. Tell an adult.

3. Try not to show fear.

4. Make the best choice.

5. After the situation, process with an adult.

REPLACEMENT SKILLS

Lesson 61: Making Positive Statements About Self

Objective: Students will list their attributes.

Materials Needed: Poster board.

Establish the Need: Read this story: *"Jeffrey was feeling very sad because his best friend had moved away. He thought no one else would ever ask him to play soccer, fish, or ride bikes in the park. He couldn't think of any reason anyone would want to be his friend."* (1) Does everyone have only bad things about them? (2) What might be some of Jeffrey's good qualities?

Procedures:

Step 1: Model the skill:

List on the board your good qualities using "Think Aloud" strategies.

1. What do I do well?
2. What do I like about my personality?
3. What do other people like about me?

Helpful Hints: You might have each student give a compliment to the person on his or her right.

Step 2: Role play with feedback:

A. Have your students state one thing good about themselves.

B. Have others write one good thing about each student.

Helpful Hints: For students with low self-esteem, affirmations are helpful. Say something positive, i.e., "I am good at making friends," aloud to your self daily while looking in mirror for six weeks. What happens if you can't find anything nice to say about yourself?

Step 3: Transfer training:

A. **School:** What am I good at in school?

B. **Home/Community:** At home, what am I good at?

C. **Peers:** What makes me a good friend?

Comments: Students often waiver between boasting and self-deprecating. Our aim is for students to make honest, positive self-statements.

Extended Activities: (1) Draw a picture of yourself showing things you are good at. (2) Journal about the things you like best about yourself. (3) Pair students and have them say three things they like about the other person. (4) Have your students list at last ten things they like about themselves. "I'm Great Award," page 164 and "Homework Form" page 14.

Lesson 61: Making Positive Statements About Self

1. What do I do well?

2. What do I like about my personality?

3. What do other people like about me?

friendly, nice smile, helpful

SELF-ACCEPTANCE

"I'm Great"

Award to

_____

for using the skill of

_____

Date _____

Signed _____

Lesson 62: Expressing Enthusiasm

Objective: Students will express enthusiasm for activities they enjoy.

Materials Needed: Board games.

Establish the Need: Read this story: *"Emily was a happy, cheerful person. She was always encouraging others and complimenting them for their effort. During soccer practice, Emily cheered loudly for her teammates and laughed and talked with everyone. Robert was very good at soccer, but he never smiled, or cheered, or acted like he was enjoying himself. When it came time to pick teams, Emily got picked, but Robert didn't because everyone thought he didn't like playing."* (1) What does being enthusiastic mean? (2) What are some consequences for being enthusiastic or not being enthusiastic?

Procedures:

Step 1: Model the skill:

Model using "Think Aloud" strategies—being enthusiastic about activities.

1. Say something positive about the activity.
2. Encourage and support others.
3. Smile and use eye contact.

Helpful Hints: Brainstorm statements which could indicate enthusiasm. (We can do it! Good job! Great! I like to play!)

Step 2: Role play with feedback:

A. Using simple board games, have your students role play being enthusiastic about playing and about others' efforts.

B. Role play expressing enthusiasm about getting a good grade.

Helpful Hints: Stress the need to be sincere. Try being a "sour puss" and see how many people like you.

Step 3: Transfer training:

A. **School:** Ask the computer teacher to reinforce appropriate enthusiasm.

B. **Home/Community:** Express enthusiasm to some member of your family. Report back.

C. **Peers:** Express enthusiasm to one person at recess. Report back.

Comments: Expressing enthusiasm can sometimes replace more self-defeating talking.

Extended Activities: (1) Journal situations in which I can be enthusiastic. (2) Name a person you see as enthusiastic. What does that person do to be enthusiastic? Discuss. Do people like to be around enthusiastic people? "I'm Great Award," page 164 and "Homework Form," page 14.

Self Acceptance

Lesson 62: Expressing Enthusiasm

1. Say something positive about the activity.

2. Encourage and support others.

3. Smile and use eye contact.

SELF-ACCEPTANCE

Lesson 63: Recognizing Likes and Differences with Your Peers

Objective: Students will list ways they are alike and different from classmates.

Materials Needed: Puppets and materials for collage.

Establish the Need: Read this story: *"Becky always tried to be like her friends. If they got their hair cut, so did she. If they wore the "grunge" look, so did she. She liked the music and food they liked. One day her friends were talking about Becky's birthday and what they might do that she would like, but none of them could think of anything that Becky seemed to like herself."* (1) Is anyone just like everyone else? (2) Why is it important to be ourselves?

Procedures:

Step 1: Model the skill:

Model using "Think Aloud" strategies—the way you are like and different.

1. How am I like others?
2. How am I different?

Helpful Hints: Since this is the age where peer emulation is gaining strength, it is important to discuss the importance of differences.

Step 2: Role play with feedback:

A. Have your students list ways they are like others and ways they are different from others. Discuss in pairs.

B. Are your friends more like you or different? Discuss.

Helpful Hints: Discuss what can happen when people try too hard to be like others. (Loss of identity, make poor choices, lose idea of what you want to be and do.) Pretend you only like people like you and don't recognize differences. Discuss the results.

Step 3: Transfer training:

A. **School:** How is our school different and like (a neighboring school)?

B. **Home/Community:** How is my family like and different from others?

C. **Peers:** How am I like and different from my friends?

Comments: This is a good time to bring up significant differences like physical and cognitive disabilities. Your school counselor is a good resource.

Extended Activities: (1) Arrange for a puppet play demonstrating physical, cognitive, and racial difference and likeness. (2) Do individual collages of likes and differences and discuss how important those qualities are to the overall class. "I'm Great Award," page 164 and "Homework Form," page 14.

Self Acceptance

Lesson 63: Recognizing Likes and Differences with Your Peers

1. How am I like others?

2. How am I different?

SELF-ACCEPTANCE

Lesson 64: People Change and Grow

Objective: Students will identify ways they have changed in the last two years.

Materials Needed: Two photos each per student as a baby or toddler.

Establish the Need: Have your students bring baby or toddler photos. Keep their identities secret. Number each and display them on the bulletin board. Have your students view the photos and try to identify each.

Procedures:

Step 1: Model the skill:

Model using "Think Aloud" strategies—how you have changed in last year, five years, 20 years?

How have I changed?

Helpful Hints: Sometimes children hang on to their sameness for stability, but it is important for them to realize everything changes.

Step 2: Role play with feedback:

A. Have your students write ways they have changed since first grade.

B. Role play how getting older helps develop personality.

Helpful Hints: Be sure your students consider physical qualities, skill level, friend making, independence, and so forth. Discuss what would happen if we didn't change.

Step 3: Transfer training:

A. **School:** How has school changed in the last five years?

B. **Home/Community:** How has my family changed since I was a baby?

C. **Peers:** How have my friendships changed?

Helpful Hints: Help your students see that change is less scary if they take an active role in it.

Comments: Some relationships will be with the same people, but change in quality.

Extended Activities: (1) Have your school counselor present a discussion on ways families change, i.e., death, divorce, relocation, children leaving home. (2) Draw a picture of my family ten years ago and today. Write about my feelings regarding those changes. "I'm Great Award," page 164 and "Homework Form," page 14.

Lesson 64: People Change and Grow

How have I changed?

SELF-ACCEPTANCE

Lesson 65: Making Mistakes—
A Learning Experience

Objective: Students will admit mistake and state what they could learn from it.

Materials Needed: Clay.

Establish the Need: Read this story: *"Martha meant to study for her spelling test, but there was a good program on TV the night before. She got an F on her test. She sulked all day and yelled at her best friend at recess. She didn't do her seat work during math because she thought, Why work when I just get F's anyway."* (1) Why did Martha fail the test? (2) What could she do in the future to prevent failing? (3) Do you think she learned from her mistake?

Procedures:

Step 1: Model the skill:

Model using "Think Aloud" strategies—getting a ticket for not having current license plates.

　　1. Why did I fail? (Bad luck, lack of effort or skill.)

　　2. How do I respond? (Good, bad, indifferent.)

　　3. What can I do next time?

Helpful Hints: It is important for your students to see that anger may be appropriate to feel, but it won't help them learn from their mistakes.

Step 2: Role play with feedback:

A. Create scenarios of failure and have them role play using "Think Aloud" strategies.

B. After you lied to your friend, you apologize. Discuss.

Helpful Hints: This is a good time to help your students accept self-responsibility and not blame when they could do something to prevent failure. Role play a mistake you made, but instead of benefiting from it, you keep doing the same mistake over and over.

Step 3: Transfer training:

A. **School:** Ask the P.E. teacher to assist your students to practice this in competitive games and/or challenging individual activities.

B. **Home/Community:** You fail to pass the swimming test to go up to the next group. What do you do?

C. **Peers:** You want to be friends with a certain group, but they refuse you. What do you do? Discuss.

Comments: In many instances we have control over succeeding or failing, but not always. Help your students see other options when they cannot control the outcome.

Extended Activities: (1) Elicit discussion of cases in literature or history when someone failed and learned from that failure. (2) Discuss the quote, "It's not whether you win or lose, but how you play the game." (3) Schedule some cooperative, not competitive games to play. (4) Use clay to attempt to make something, fail, and reshape. "I'm Great Award," page 164 and "Homework Form," page 14.

Self Acceptance

Lesson 65: Making Mistakes: A Learning Experience

1. Why did I fail? (Bad luck, lack of effort or skill.)

2. How do I respond? (Good, bad, indifferent.)

3. What can I do next time?

SELF-ACCEPTANCE

Dennis Hanken, Ed.S. and Judith Kennedy, Ed.S.

Lesson 66: Handling "Put Downs"

Objective: Students will eliminate "put downs" (negative statements) of self and others.

Materials Needed: None.

Establish the Need: Read this story: *"Karen seemed to take any opportunity to tell people they were stupid, or couldn't do an activity, or wore funny clothes. She had a group of friends, and when she would start putting down a person, her friends joined in. Other kids tried to avoid her, but she still hurt a lot of people."* (1) How do you feel about a person who "puts you down?" (2) Why do you suppose Karen does this? (3) What could she do instead?

Procedures:

Step 1: Model the skill:

Model using "Think Aloud" strategies—handling the "put downs" of a coworker.

1. Is what the person says true?
2. What can I do?
   a. Ignore.
   b. Speak up.
   c. Avoid.
   d. Walk away.

Helpful Hints: Help your students see that "put downs" are spoken by people who do not feel good about themselves.

Step 2: Role play with feedback:

A. Create scenarios in which students experience "put downs" and have them role play with feedback using "Think Aloud" strategies.

B. Role play "put downs" during a football game. Discuss.

Helpful Hints: Your students will probably have had a lot of exposure to "put downs;" they will just need assistance in handling them.

Step 3: Transfer training:

A. **School:** Ask other teachers to watch for "put downs" and reinforce appropriate handling of them.

B. **Home/Community:** Ask your students to observe "put downs" in their environment. Report back and discuss.

C. **Peers:** Make a contract with your students in class that they will not say "put downs" to fellow classmates.

Comments: Helping students to feel good about themselves will help eliminate "putting down" others.

Extended Activities: (1) Journal: how do I feel when people "put me down?" (2) Develop a skit showing "put downs" and appropriate handling of them. "I'm Great Award," page 164 and "Homework Form," page 14.

Self Acceptance

Lesson 66: Handling "Put Downs"

1. Is what the person says true?

2. What can I do?

a. Ignore.

b. Speak up.

c. Avoid.

d. Walk away.

SELF-ACCEPTANCE

Dennis Hanken, Ed.S. and Judith Kennedy, Ed.S.

Lesson 67: Doing Your Best is Important

Objective: Students will try to do task that is difficult for them.

Materials Needed: Saucers and coins.

Establish the Need: Have your students attempt something very difficult, such as getting a coin in a saucer from six feet away. Discuss with them how they felt when they tried. When they failed. When they succeeded.

Procedures:

Step 1: Model the skill:

Model using "Think Aloud" strategies—doing something difficult, such as balancing a pencil on one finger vertically or juggling three objects.

1. Can I do the task?
2. What will happen if I try?
3. Try my best!

Helpful Hints: Discuss with your students the fun and challenge of attempting tasks with which they may have difficulty.

Step 2: Role play with feedback:

A. Have your students role play trying something hard and doing their best. Might use new math concept, map activity, physical activity like balancing on one foot with their eyes closed, or a new game.

B. You go out for some sport, do your best, but you get cut. Discuss.

Helpful Hints: Discuss with your students how new discoveries throughout history have been a result of trying, failing, and trying some more. For contrast when you try out for a sport, don't try your best. What are the results?

Step 3: Transfer training:

A. **School:** Ask the P.E. teacher to reinforce trying to do your best.

B. **Home/Community:** Ask the parents to reinforce trying to do your best on chores and activities.

C. **Peers:** Report to class something you have learned to do which was difficult at first.

Comments: Now is a good time to discuss that everyone is good at some things and not as good at others.

Extended Activities: (1) Ask the counselor to discuss the challenges that people with disabilities face to do even everyday tasks and/or show a video showing Special Olympic athletes trying their best. (2) Research people in history who have succeeded despite difficulties because they tried to do their best. "I'm Great Award," page 164 and "Homework Form," page 14.

Self Acceptance

Lesson 67: Doing Your Best is Important

1. Can I do the task?

2. What will happen if I try?

3. Try my best!

SELF-ACCEPTANCE

Dennis Hanken, Ed.S. and Judith Kennedy, Ed.S.

Lesson 68: "Put Ups"

Objective: Students will state "put ups" (positive statements) to self and others.

Materials Needed: Journals.

Establish the Need: Read this story: *"Jeff seemed to always see the best in other people. He would say 'Good job!' to others who completed a task, and 'Nice try' to people who made a mistake while trying. Other students always seemed to feel better when he was around."* (1) Why did students like to be around Jeff? (2) What is a "put up."

Procedures:

Step 1: Model the skill:

Model using "Think Aloud" strategies—giving a "put up" to every member of the class.

1. What can I honestly say that I like about the person?
2. Do it.

Helpful Hints: Unfortunately your students will not always have been exposed to saying or hearing positive statements. Be a role model for them.

Step 2: Role play with feedback:

A. In groups, have your students take turns giving each other a "put up."

B. Have your students give teacher "put ups" and vice versa. Discuss.

Helpful Hints: Have them give a "put up" to self. Which is more damaging, "put ups" or "put downs?"

Step 3: Transfer training:

A. **School:** Ask the school staff to give your class "put ups" for the next four weeks.

B. **Home/Community:** Send note to parents asking them to give "put ups" to their children.

C. **Peers:** Assign every student to give three "put ups" each day to other persons.

Comments: Research states that children and adults learn best and flourish in environments that have at least five positive statements for every one negative.

Extended Activities: (1) Journal on how you feel when you get "put downs" and "put ups." (2) Create a skit showing the power of "put ups" to be used for lower grades. (3) Create a game incorporating giving opponents "put ups" at every play. "I'm Great Award," page 164 and "Homework Form," page 14.

Self Acceptance

Lesson 68: "Put Ups"

1. What can I honestly say that I like about the person?

2. Do it.

SELF-ACCEPTANCE

Dennis Hanken, Ed.S. and Judith Kennedy, Ed.S.

Bibliography

Periodical

Fleming, D.C., Ritchie, B., & Fleming, E.R. (Spring, 1983). "Fostering the Social Adjustment of Disturbed Students." Teaching *Exceptional Children,* 172-175.

Gresham, F.M. (February, 1982). "Misguided Mainstreaming: The Case for Social Skills Training with Handicapped Children." *Exceptional Children,* 422-431.

Pekarik, E.G., Prinz, R.J., & Weintraub, D.E., Sheldon, & Neale, J.M. (1976). "A Sociometric Technique for Assessing Children's Social Behavior." *Journal of Abnormal Child Psychology,* 4, 1, 83-97.

Rutherford, Robert B. (July, 1997). "Why Doesn't Social Skills Training Work?" *Council for Exceptional Children,* 14.

Books

Aesop. (1993). *Aesop's fables.* New York: Grosset & Dunlap.

Bellack, A.S., & Morrison, R.L. (1982). "Interpersonal Dysfunction" in *International handbook of behavior modification and therapy.* New York & London: Penum Press., 717-743.

Brockman, M.P. (1985). "Best Practices in Assessment of Social Skills and Peer Interaction" in *Best practices in school psychology.* Kent, OH: National Association of School Psychologists, 43-609.

Frank, R.A., & Edwards, P.P. (1993). *Building self-esteem.* Portland, OR: Ednick Communications.

Cartledge, G., & Fellows Milburn, J. (1986). *Teaching social skills to children.* Needham heights, MA: Allyn & Bacon.

Gresham, F.M. "Best Practice in Social Skills Training" in *Best practices in school psychology.* Kent, OH: National Association of School Psychologists, 181-192.

Huggins, P., Wood Manion, D., & Moen, L. (1993). *Teaching friendship skills: Intermediation version.* Longmont, CO: Sopris West.

Madaras, L. (1993). *My feelings, my self.* New York: Newmarket.

McCarney, S.B. (1989). *Attention deficit disorders intervention manual.* Columbia, MO: Hawthorne.

McGinnis, E., & Goldstein, A.P. (1984). *Skillstreaming the elementary school child.* Champaign, IL: Research.

Rich, D. (1992). *Megaskills.* New York: Houghton Mifflin.

Vernon, A. (1989). *Thinking, feeling, and behaving.* Champaign, IL: Research.